Table of Contents

Part I
HTML Web Design

Chapter 1

Introduction to HTML

Introduction

HTML is the first place to start when building a webpage. With this application, you usually consider two distinguished parts of Web design. First, you will create a webpage which should be really attractive in the eyes of the customers or users (webpage layout). Secondly, you need to deal with the server-side which will be able to communicate with your client-side. HTML performs on the client-side. The client-side is the side with which users or clients interact. To start learning web design and development you must begin using HTML. It is very easy to learn and you do not need to compile it in the same way as programming languages. In fact, you do not need prior knowledge of any programming languages. HTML is a script language means that it is almost the same as typing in a basic editor. There are some fundamental and well understood tags that you can easily remember. In this chapter you will learn the basic tags of HTML, how to write simple scripts and how to run your HTML codes. Each tag is followed by clear examples.

HTML is really easy; you can learn it in less than 2 weeks!

Basic understanding of HTML

HTML is a unique, easy language (script) used to create WebPages. Sometimes students ask where they should start in order to become a web programmer. The answer is clearly HTML. In fact, HTML is the basis for all web scripting languages. In reality, all web programming languages such as PHP, ASP, .NET and JSP use only HTML codes. HTML stands for **H**yper **T**ext **M**arkup Language. The HTML is just a text and nothing else. You type some text and then design it with different colors, fonts and styles. HTML is not a high level language like **JAVA** or **C++**; rather it is a *script* language which does not need to be compiled prior to running. HTML and JavaScript are both client-side applications. So what is the client-side? The client-side is everything you see on your website from your computer. On the other hand, you may need the server-side for real business or even personal websites. So what is the server-side? The server- side is designed to respond the demands of the client. Let's make this simpler with an example: Suppose you want to buy a book online from Amazon. You will choose your book and input such personal information as your name, address and credit card number. Then you will see the price, tax, the cost of shipping and finally the total amount. Remember that you have not yet entered the cost of shipping or the tax-rate. The sever-side looks at the information and calculates the related amount so that you will see the total amount on your screen.

▶ **Note** that the server is not beside you, but rather is probably situated in another city or another country, depending on where you rented it. You have access to it through your Internet connection.

In short, your request goes through the server and back again to you with an answer.

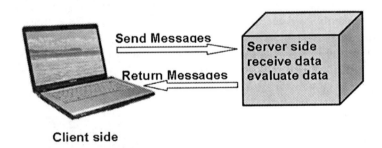

Client side

When you register online and fill out a form on a webpage, all the information will be saved on the database inside the server.

Why do I need databases?

If you have a website that has to handle data from your clients, you need to create databases in the server-side. If you sell something online, people must log in and enter their personal information and then all of that information must be saved in your database. The database allows you to collect data from different sources. For example, book sellers may want to keep some data from their customers such as their ID, names, telephone number, title, price and address.

At this point you do not need to be worry about database and table creation.

Sample of Table in database(SQL SERVER)

	ID	Names	Tel	Title	price
1	2536	Patrick Lomomba	258147	Java programming	55.75
2	4545	Quam NeKromeh	589574	Ajax	75.75
3	2545	Alam Shangi	968574	JavaScript	35.25
4	2549	Dolmeh Badenjan	452368	PHP	63.25
5	2555	Tebooli Lebnani	558899	MySQL	35.25

You can see that all the data has been stored inside the table in your database. Here we entered some small data, but in reality the tables and databases are very big. If there are many people purchasing online from your company (10000 people per month), then you will have several tables and databases. All information will be saved into databases. The database not only stores the data, but allows you to manipulate the data and see different results. For example, if you want to know all the prices greater than $50, you could write a statement similar to this:

*select * from client where price>50*

Why HTML?

Why should we learn HTML? There are many programs on the market such as *Dreamweaver*, *Flash*, *GoLive* and many other tools which make it seem like there is no need to learn HTML. However, the reality is that a programmer or web designer must know the mechanism of web programming. The ready-made **IDE** does help you to create a website, but its abilities are limited. Consequently, you need to have knowledge of script programming. The *IDE* tools generate very long codes and lower the speed of websites. You will later see how knowledge of HTML helps you to customize your website. You will also need to learn *JavaScript* to make your website more dynamic. We will introduce some tools that will help you to create animation, logos, buttons, fancy colors and various fonts.

Starting HTML

What do you need? You only need a text-editor and browser such as Internet Explorer (**IE**) or Mozilla-Firefox. If you are connected to the Internet then you probably have one of these browsers. You can use any editor you like **Notepad** or **Textpad**. In fact, HTML is editor free meaning you can use any text editor you want. HTML is a collection of tags which you may need to memorize them. What is a tag? A tag is a special character which contains the HTML command that tells the browser what to do. The HTML tag looks like this sign **< >** which is an open and closed tag. In fact, it is just like the "*less than*" and "*greater than*" mathematical operators.

> ▶ **Note:** If you do not have a browser or a good browser, you can simply download (for free) the Firefox browser from **Mozilla.com/Firefox**

What is W3C?

W3C was created in October 1994 by Tim Berners-Lee who is the Inventor of the Web. W3C Stands for the World Wide Web Consortium (WWW) and it is working to standardize the Web. The recommendation for web design comes from W3C.

W3C is hosted by these three universities:
◆ Massachusetts Institute of Technology in the USA
◆ The French National Research Institute in Europe
◆ Keio University in Japan

Browser support

A **web browser** is a software application that enables users to display text, images, videos, music, different file formats and to interact with multimedia. There are different kinds of browsers which respond to objects differently. As the web developer you must know how to overcome the issues of various browsers. Fortunately, these days almost all browsers function in a similar way. Mozilla-Firefox and Internet Explorer are the easiest to use of all browsers.

Let's look at a simple HTML program:

> ▶ **Note:** The HTML is NOT case sensitive, so you can use lowercase or uppercase letters.

```
<HTML>
Body of program must be here
</HTML>
```

Just open your notepad and type the above code which has only two lines. However, this HTML program won't do anything. Look at the third line and you will see that the HTML tag is closed by a slash "/" like </ HTML>. You will later see that all HTML tags must be closed by such a slash. The above HTML does not have the **HEAD**, **TITLE** or **BODY** which every HTML script must have. Now we will try to create them for our program. General format of HTML script:

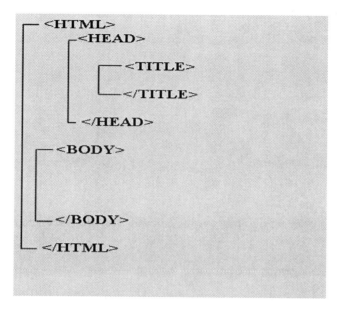

Analysis: The program starts with the <HTML> tag and by the end the tag must be closed with </HTML>. You will see the **<HEAD>** open tag and **</HEAD>** closed tag. It is important to remember that the title is situated inside the **HEAD**. In fact, along with the **TITLE** tag, the head also contains the **META** tag, which you will see later. But for now it just contains the title tag. The title tag must be closed before the head tag. The major part is the body tag in which program contents must be placed. You can see that the <HTML > tag, which started on the top of program, will be closed at the end with </HTML>.

▶ **Note:** The HEAD may contain one or all of the following:
» **TITLE**
» **META tag**
» **JavaScript**

There can be more elements like **LINK** or **CSS STYLE** under the HTML head, but those are the common elements that should be placed under the head tag. Look at the following elements which can be placed under the head:

<HEAD>
 <TITLE>The Java Tutorial</TITLE>
 <META NAME="description" CONTENT="Get knowledge about Java Programming.">
 <META NAME="keywords" CONTENT="java, tutorial, learn java, examples, book, applets, swing, JSP">
 </HEAD>

Getting started

We will try to write a small HTML program and run it to see the script output.

Example: 1.1
```
<HTML>
<HEAD>
<TITLE>First HTML Language</Title>
</HEAD>
<BODY>
This is my first HTML workshop!
</BODY>
</HTML>
```

Just open your **Notepad** or any other text-editor and type the above code.
Save it as **First.html**

Remember: the file's name is optional. You can use any name that you like, but the extension must be **html**.
Open this file in your browser or just double-click on the file under the explorer folder.
You will see this result:

On the top of the page you see "*First HTML Language*". This is your title which is indicated in your code. The "*This is my first HTML workshop!*" is indicated in the body of program.

▐▶ **Note:** Do NOT close your browser. To run your program, just click on the **refresh** button on the top of your browser.

HTML body

You must place everything you want to show on the page under the BODY of HTML. When you type some text on the body, the text will be shown as it is originally written. You must format your text to control the desired result.

Formatting text

HTML provides many tags to control the text such as BOLD, ITALIC and UNDERLINE.

Example: 1.2
```
<HTML>
<HEAD>
<TITLE>BOLD in HTML </Title>
</HEAD>
<BODY>
<b>Look at me, am I in Bold?</b>
</BODY>
</HTML>
```

The open and closed tags <b> </b> cause the text to be in bold.
Look at the output:

Look at me, am I in Bold?

Now in order to change the same text to ITALIC, use the **<I>** tag instead of the **<b>** tag.
<I>Look at me, am I in Italic?</I>
The program produces this output:

Look at me, am I in ITALIC?

You can combine different tags. For example, use ITALIC and BOLD at the same time.
Just change the code within the above program:
<I><b>Look at me; am I in ITALIC and BOLD? </b> </I>
The above code produces this output:

Look at me; am I in ITALIC and BOLD?

Line break

Suppose you want to show some text in several lines. By default the text will not return to the new line, so you must use the break tag: **
**.

Remember: Do NOT use numbers beside your code. In each example we use numbers for clarity but you must not use the number for your code.

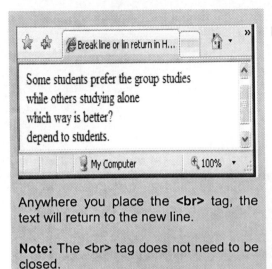

Anywhere you place the **
** tag, the text will return to the new line.

Note: The <br> tag does not need to be closed.

Example: 1.3
1. <HTML>
2. <HEAD>
3. <TITLE>Break line or line return in HTML </TITLE>
4. </HEAD>
5. <BODY>
6. Some students prefer group studies
 while others studying alone
 which way is better?
 depends on students.
7. </BODY>
8. </HTML>

Some useful HTML tags

Tag	Explanation
<b>text</b>	Make text as bold
<I>text</I>	Make text as Italic
 	New line
<hr>	Horizontal line
<u> text</u>	Underline
_{text}	Lower text
^{text}	Upper text
<strike>text</strike>	Strike text
<pre> text</pre>	Show text exactly the same as written code
<em> text</em>	The same as Italic
<strong>text<strong>	The same as Bold
<p> </P>	Set a Paragraph

We will demonstrate some tags from the above table.

DTD

You may use the **Data Type Definition (DTD)** for each example. Each example contains the DTD on the top. Without DTD you can't validate your code. You will see using and validating DTD in the HTML, CSS and XHTML parts. According to HTML standards, each

HTML document requires a *document type declaration* (DTD). The "*DOCTYPE*" tells *validator* what version of HTML is to be used.

The most common use of DOCTYPE in HTML is:
<!DOCTYPE HTML PUBLIC "-//W3C//DTD HTML 4.01//EN"
"http://www.w3.org/TR/html4/strict.dtd">

Instead of **strict.dtd**, try to use **Transitional.dtd** which is more flexible in using different browsers. We use **Transitional** when our users have old browsers. We use **Strict** when we want to use the **CSS** and restricted to the new browsers, it may create problems for old browsers users. We use **Frameset** when the HTML frame has been used. You do also need to use **charset** encoding in HTML. The *charset* must be placed inside the head.
<meta http-equiv="Content-Type" content="text/html; **charset**=iso-8859-1">
The default charset in HTML is ISO-8859-1, which is an 8-bit Western European character set, for other languages consult the charset encoding languages.

Example: 1.4
1. <!DOCTYPE HTML PUBLIC "-//W3C//DTD HTML 4.01//EN"
2. "http://www.w3.org/TR/html4/Strict.dtd">
3. <head>
4. <meta http-equiv="Content-Type" content="text/html; charset=iso-8859-1">
5. <title>HTML Tags</title>
6. </head>
7. <body>
8. <p>
9. <i>History</i> is helping us to our <b>futures</b> and to not make a _{Mistake}
10. </p>
11. </body>
12. </html>

You can see that the <I> causes HISTORY to be Italic. The <b> tag is affecting the word FUTURE to be in bold and the <sub> tag makes the word Mistake to be in Subscript.
The above program is validated by http://validator.w3.org which is from W3C and upon validating you see an icon.

Here a sample of validator:

Validate by URI   **Validate by File Upload**   **Validate by Direct Input**

Validate by File Upload

Upload a document for validation:

File: `D:\Example1-4.html`   Browse...

▸ More Options

(Check)

You can use the below icon which tells you that your code is validated. In fact there are several validators, you may use one of them for you code.

HTML comments

Why should we use a comment in our source? Using comments in HTML is optional but sometimes you need to use them. For instance, you want clarify some part of your code or you want to describe your personal information or information about your company, as the creator of this website.

The comments are placed in the source code, but the compiler disregards them. Therefore, they will not be displayed on the page output.

There are several ways to put your code into comments with HTML.
These are all legal comments:

- **<!---->**
- **<!-- TEXT -->**
- **<!-- TEXT -- ---- TEXT-->**
- **<!------ TEXT -->**

However, the different browsers occasionally generate errors with some of these comments. Some web developers use comments for their line separator such as
<!---------------------------->. This can be wrong because it has to be a multiple of the number 4.

The best, problem-free comment is
<!--   -->

You can see that it starts with an open tag, followed by an inclination sign and two little dashes. It is then ended by two little dashes with a closed tag.

Example: 1.5
1. <!DOCTYPE HTML PUBLIC "-//W3C//DTD HTML 4.01//EN"
2. "http://www.w3.org/TR/html4/Strict.dtd">
3. <head>
4. <meta http-equiv="Content-Type" content="text/html; charset=iso-8859-1">
5. <title>HTML Comments</title>
6. </head>
7. <body>
8. <p>
9. <!--
10. This side is written on January 2008 for those who really want to learn HTML and become a web designer.
11. -->
12. We try to make HTML as easy as possible!
13. Just look at the examples then evaluate the level of ease!
14. </p>
15. </body>
16. </html>

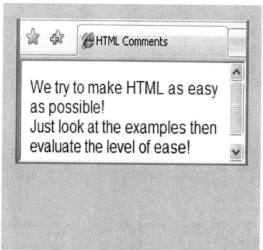

In this example, we use some text as comments, but you can see that this text has not shown up on our program output.

<!-- This side is written on January for those who really want to learn HTML and become a web designer -->

Wait a minute! Why should I use comment when it is not shown on screen? The reality a programmer is using a comment for himself or for others that may use this code.
You can use comments anywhere inside the HTML code.

Review questions

1-HTML stands for:

2-What is a tag in HTML?

3-The tag for return new line is
        True   False

4-The <b> bold tag does not need to be closed. True   False

5-<i>Carwash</i> How will this word be shown on the browser?

6-Can two or more tags be combined?   Yes   No

7-What is the difference between <SUB> and <SUP>?

8- In what situation do we usually use the <PRE> tag.

9- Which elements must usually be placed inside the HEAD?

10-Where will Title be shown?

Answers

1-HyperText Markup Language

2-Tag used to format the text.

3-True

4-False

5-Italic

6-Yes

7-Text goes down with SUB and it goes up with SUP. In both cases the *text becomes small.*

8-When we want text be shown as it is written in the source code, such as for poetry.

9-Title, Meta tag and JavaScript

10-On the top of the page at the title bar

Chapter 2

Formatting Texts

Introduction

HTML has the capacity to provide nice and efficient text formatting. In fact, it formats texts with the minimum tags required. We can simply use align tag to place text in three general places: left, right, and center. It also explains the way to use top and bottom areas. You can use the <HR> tag to draw a line-separator, and use <UL> and <OL> to deal with ordered and unordered lists. In this chapter we will demonstrate the basic text formatting with the related examples. The examples are able describe everything with minimum explanation.

Heading

In the previous chapter, we mentioned the importance of HTML body. You will place everything you want to see on your webpage under the body of HTML program. You can simply change the size of your text by using heading. The tag for heading is just an open tag <H1> and a closed tag</H1>. There are six headings that affect the text size. The smaller the heading level number, the larger the print size:

<H1> Heading #1 </H1>   *Larger text*
<H2> Heading #2 </H2>
<H3> Heading #3 </H3>
<H4> Heading #4 </H4>
<H5> Heading #5 </H5>
<H6> Heading #6 </H6>   *Smaller text*

Example: 2.1

```
<!DOCTYPE HTML PUBLIC "-//W3C//DTD HTML 4.01//EN"
"http://www.w3.org/TR/html4/Strict.dtd">
 <head>
 <meta http-equiv="Content-Type" content="text/html; charset=iso-8859-1">
<title>HEADING </title>
</head>
<body>
<H1> Heading #1 </H1>
<H2> Heading #2 </H2>
<H3> Heading #3 </H3>
<H4> Heading #4 </H4>
<H5> Heading #5 </H5>
<H6> Heading #6 </H6>
</body>
</html>
```

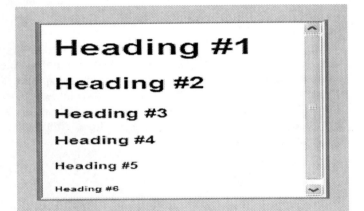

The heading automatically returns the new-line. Therefore, you do not need a line-break to use the <br> tag.

▶ **Note:** Headings are always in **bold**.

Attributes

Attributes are used to design the text. When your website is loading, the browser is looking for attributes. For example, it is looking for alignments which might be set to **center**, **left**, **right** and **justify**.

➤ **Note:** many HTML attributes are **deprecated** means no longer useable in modern browsers. One of these attributes is align which suppose to make alignment in text like: left, center and right, but it does not supported anymore. Check out this example.

Example: 2.2
```
1.  <!DOCTYPE HTML PUBLIC "-//W3C//DTD HTML 4.01//EN"
2.  "http://www.w3.org/TR/html4/Strict.dtd">
3.  <head>
4.  <meta http-equiv="Content-Type" content="text/html; charset=iso-8859-1">
5.  <title>Text Align </title>
6.  </head>
7.  <body>
8.  <H2 align="left"> Am I aligned left?</H2>
9.  <H2 align="center"> Am I in the center?</H2>
10. <H2 align="right"> Am I aligned right?</H2>
11. </body>
12. </HTML>
```

It works under (Internet Explorer) **IE** browser but when you try validating the above example, it generates **wrong message**.

❸ *Line 8, Column 10:* **there is no attribute "ALIGN"**.

```
<H2 align="left"> Am I aligned left?</H2>
```

Later we will use CSS (Cascading Style Sheet) to solve the problem. For example we use this style.
```
<STYLE type="text/css">
 H1 { text-align: left; text-align: center;  text-align: right;}
 </STYLE>
```
But don't worry at this point we will discuss CSS topics on chapter four.

Paragraph
Text formatting may require several paragraphs. A paragraph is a tag like <P> </P>. This pair of tags forces the text to behave as a paragraph.

Example: 2.3
```
1.  <!DOCTYPE HTML PUBLIC "-//W3C//DTD HTML 4.01//EN"
2.  "http://www.w3.org/TR/html4/Strict.dtd">
3.  <head>
4.  <meta http-equiv="Content-Type" content="text/html; charset=iso-8859-1">
5.  <title> Paragraph </title>
6.  </head>
7.  <BODY>
8.  <P>
```

```
9.  Books choose their authors; the act of creation<br>
10. is not entirely a rational and conscious one.<br>
11. <b>Salman Rushdie</b>
12. </P>
13. <P>
14. 'Unfortunately many young writers are <br>
15. more concerned with fame than with their<br>
16. own work... It's much more important<br>
17. to write than to be written about.'<br>
18. <b>Gabriel Garcia Marquez</b>
19. </P>
20. </BODY>
21. </HTML>
```

As you can see, we are still using break <br> tags to force the line to the new line. The <P> tag inserts a blank line on the top, just after the <p> tag is declared and another blank line on the bottom, just before the tag is closed.
We used the <b> bold tag inside the <P> tag to print the name in bold to be more visible.

> **Note:** The browser automatically inserts a blank line on the top and bottom of the paragraph.

Paragraph Justification

The attributes allow for the justification of the paragraph. You may think of left or right justification when you want to print text on the browser. The justification of booth side which is using <align="justify">tag is not validate HTML code and it is deprecated, but if run this code you will still get the result.

```
<HTML>
<HEAD><TITLE>Justification</TITLE> </HEAD>
<BODY>
<p align="justify">
```
There are some books that refuse to be written. They stand their ground year after year and will not be persuaded. It isn't because the book is not there and worth being written --

it is only because the right form of the story does not present itself. There is only one right form for a story and if you fail to find that form the story will not tell itself.
<b>Mark Twain</b>
</p>
</BODY> </HTML>

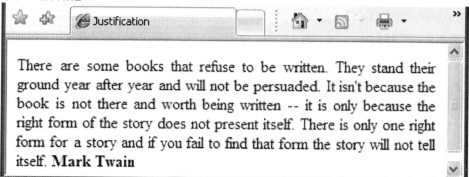

We did not use any <br> tags on the source code. The text is well justified from the left and the right.

If you change the align attribute to left or right then you see the different results. For example, this is aligned to the right. We will later using CSS.

Horizontal line

As its name implies, the horizontal tag draws a line across the screen and is identified by the <HR> tag. In fact, this is good for the separation of two parts of a text, or it can be used to put some text in a different format.

▶ **Note:** There is no need to close the <HR/> tag.

Example: 2.4

```
1.  <!DOCTYPE HTML PUBLIC "-//W3C//DTD HTML 4.01//EN"
2.  "http://www.w3.org/TR/html4/Strict.dtd">
3.  <head>
4.  <meta http-equiv="Content-Type" content="text/html; charset=iso-8859-1">
5.  <title> HORZONTAL Line </title>
6.  </head>
7.  <BODY><div>
8.  Am I sitting on a HORIZONTAL line?
9.  <HR> Am I sitting between two HORIZONTAL lines?
10. <HR>
11. There are two HORIZONTAL lines after me!
12. <HR>
13. <HR></div>
14. </body>
15. </HTML>
```

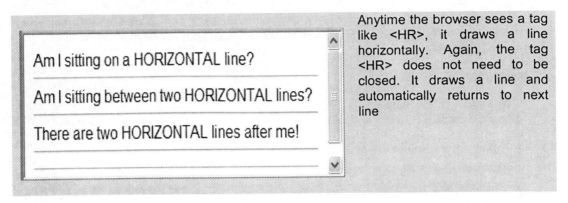

Anytime the browser sees a tag like <HR>, it draws a line horizontally. Again, the tag <HR> does not need to be closed. It draws a line and automatically returns to next line

Lists

You might want to use the list in order to further design HTML text. The list allows you to organize your data or texts within your webpage. There are different types of lists in HTML.

- <ul> Unordered prints bullets
- <ol> Ordered prints number
- <dl> definition - Dictionary

Ordered list

We use the <OL> tag to print out ordered-lists. Inside **OL**, you must use the <LI> tag which forces a list to be printed by leading an ordered number starting from 1.

Example: 2.5
```
<!DOCTYPE HTML PUBLIC "-//W3C//DTD HTML 4.01//EN"
"http://www.w3.org/TR/html4/Strict.dtd">
 <head>
 <meta http-equiv="Content-Type" content="text/html; charset=iso-8859-1">
<title> Ordered list</title>
</head>
<BODY>
<ol>
<li> Bananas</li>
<li> Apples</li>
<li> Grapes</li>
</ol>
</BODY>
</HTML>
```

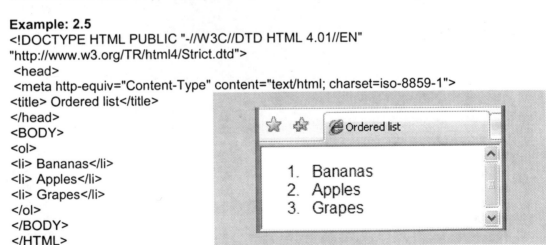

The ordered list prints out the list in numerical order. It starts from 1 and increases by 1 until the end of the list.

You may want the numbers to print-out starting from a different number, such as the number 3, and then to continue until the end of the list. We can make the list do just that. Use this tag **<ol start = "3" >** at the beginning of the list. But remember the start attribute is also **deprecated**.

List in Roman or Letters

If you would like to further manipulate the ordered-list by, for example, using Roman (I, II,..V) or letter (A, B ... Z) formats instead of generic numbers, you just use the attribute on the top.

Remember: It can be done in both lowercase and uppercase formats.

Example: 2.7
1. <!DOCTYPE HTML PUBLIC "-//W3C//DTD HTML 4.01 Transitional//EN" "http://www.w3.org/TR/html4/loose.dtd">
2. <head>
3. <meta http-equiv="Content-Type" content="text/html; charset=iso-8859-1">
4. <title> Roman Number List</title>
5. </head>
6. <body>
7. <ol type="i">
8. <li> Bananas</li>
9. <li> Apples</li>
10. <li> Grapes</li>
11. <li> Oranges</li>
12. <li> Tomatoes</li>
13. <li> Potatoes</li>
14. </ol>
15. </body>
16. </html>

Remember: we use **Transitional.dtd**, simply because the Type attribute is deprecated. The transitional.dtd is used for old browser and there is not restriction.

<ol type="1"> Numeral order
<ol type="i"> Roman lowercase
<ol type="I"> Roman uppercase
<ol type="A"> Letter uppercase
<ol type="i"> Letter lowercase

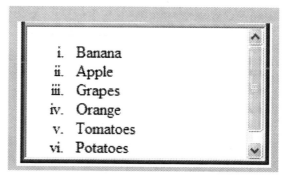

Try to change the <ol type="l"> to <ol type="a"> or "A" and you will see the order change from Roman to alphabetical order.

	Letter lowercase		**Letter uppercase**
a.	Bananas	A.	Bananas
b.	Apples	B.	Apples
c.	Grapes	C.	Grapes
d.	Oranges	D.	Oranges
e.	Tomatoes	E.	Tomatoes
f.	Potatoes	F.	Potatoes

	Numeral		**Roman Lowercase**		**Roman Uppercase**
1.	Bananas	i.	Bananas	I.	Bananas
2.	Apples	ii.	Apples	II.	Apples
3.	Grapes	iii.	Grapes	III.	Grapes
4.	Oranges	iv.	Oranges	IV.	Oranges
5.	Tomatoes	v.	Tomatoes	V.	Tomatoes
6.	Potatoes	vi.	Potatoes	VI.	Potatoes

Unordered lists

Unlike the ordered-list, which is managed by an order of numeral, Roman and letter, the unordered list inserts bullets in front of the list elements. There are three unordered list signs: Square, Disc, and circle. The bullet disc prints out by default.

Example: 2.8
```
<!DOCTYPE HTML PUBLIC "-//W3C//DTD HTML 4.01//EN"
"http://www.w3.org/TR/html4/Strict.dtd">
<head>
<meta http-equiv="Content-Type" content="text/html; charset=iso-8859-1">

<title> Unordered list</title>
</head>
<BODY>
<ul>
<li> Toyota Camry</li>
<li> Toyota Corolla </li>
<li>Toyota Lexus </li>
</ul>
</BODY>
</HTML>
```

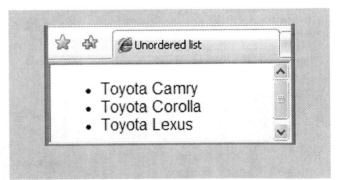

This is the default unordered list which generates a disc beside each element in the list. However, there is no order. All elements have the same priority.

Now you can change the unordered list to print out the desired bullet. We can use three forms of unordered lists. They are as follows:

<UL TYPE="disc">
<UL TYPE="square">
<UL TYPE="circle">

Change the above program to one of these bullet formats, and use *Transitional.dtd*. It produces these forms:

<UL TYPE="disc"> default	<UL TYPE="square">	<UL TYPE="circle">
• Camry • Corolla • Lexus	▪ Camry ▪ Corolla ▪ Lexus	○ Camry ○ Corolla ○ Lexus

Multiple lists

Sometimes you want to create a multiple list which contains different, unrelated items. In this case you can create Inner and Outer lists in which one item follows another.

Example: 2.9

```
1.  <!DOCTYPE HTML PUBLIC "-//W3C//DTD HTML 4.01//EN"
2.  "http://www.w3.org/TR/html4/Strict.dtd">
3.  <head> <meta http-equiv="Content-Type" content="text/html; charset=iso-8859-1">
4.  <title>Inner and Outer list</title>
5.  </head> <body>
6.  <UL>
7.  <LI>Shopping List
8.  <UL>
9.  <LI>For Eat  <LI>Cosmetics
10. </UL>
11. <LI>Shopping list
12. <OL>
13. <LI>Inner List
14. <OL> <LI>Breads <LI>Meats </OL>
15. <LI> Outer List
16. <OL>
17. <LI> Soap <LI> Javax
18. <LI>Razor
19. <LI>Cream
20. </OL> </OL> </UL>
21. </body>
22. </html>
```

Preformatted text

We use the <PRE> tag for preformatted text. The PRE element contains *preformatted text* which browsers read as exactly as was written in the code, including the white spaces.

PRE is useful for formatting programming code, poetry, or any other text that needs white-spaces.

Example: 2.10

```
<!DOCTYPE HTML PUBLIC "-//W3C//DTD HTML 4.01//EN"
"http://www.w3.org/TR/html4/Strict.dtd">
 <head>
 <meta http-equiv="Content-Type" content="text/html; charset=iso-8859-1">
<title>HTML Pre Tags</title>
</head>
<body>
<p>
<b>The song that became a key
Anthem<br>
of the US Civil Rights Movement</b>
</p>
<pre>
1.We shall overcome some day
Oh, deep in my heart
I do believe
We shall overcome some day
2.We'll walk hand in hand
We'll walk hand in hand some day
3.We shall all be free
We shall all be free some day
4.We are not afraid
We are not afraid some day
5.We are not alone
We are not alone some day
</pre>
</body>
</html>
```

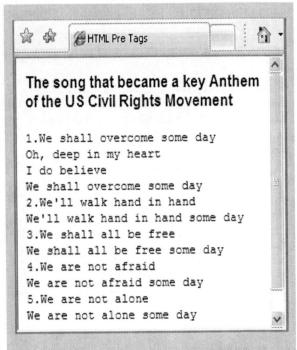

The poetry that is written within the HTML code is shown exactly as it is formatted in the source code. The browser does not change anything; therefore the code remains the same.

Review questions

1- How many forms do HTML headings provide?

2- By default the heading returns to the new line.   True   False

3- List three attributes that can be used within heading.

4- In HTML the <P> tag generates a paragraph.   True   False

5- What is the justification attribute in a paragraph?

6- You can have multiple paragraphs within HTML text.   True   False

7- <HR/> tag does not need to be closed.   True   False

8- By default unordered-lists print out Square bullets.   True   False

9- Circle bullets create an empty circle.   True   False

10- Explain how to generate Roman lowercase in an ordered list.

Answers

1- 6

2- True

3- Right, Left, Center

4- True

5- Justifies two sides of text

6- True

7- True

8- False, generate Disc bullet

9- True

10- On the top use <OL type="i">

Chapter 3

Introduction

Creating a client-side webpage is easy with HTML, but creating an attractive webpage requires a great deal of effort. Certainly text colors, background colors, fonts and styles all play very important roles. Those who know how to use colors are more successful in designing an attractive webpage. The background color simply has to be matched with the text color. You can manipulate color by using their RGB values. In this chapter we will discuss colors and fonts and how to use them in an easy way.

The elements and attributes that we are discussing in this chapter are deprecated by W3C which are not anymore applicable for modern browser users. We try to show you how we can use them in HTML. There are still old browsers that have problem with new web-design features. We will discuss the CSS in the next chapter. But try to learn these elements in this chapter. We use **Transitional.dtd** in the **DOCTYPE**.

Fonts

In the previous chapter we looked at different sizes of *heading*. The heading is limited to 6 different sizes and each size is fixed. An example of this is from 24 points for <H1> to 8 points for <H6>. What happens if you want to use a family font which gives you more selection? In HTML we use the **<font>** tag. However, this tag has been deprecated so we must use CSS.

▮▶ **Note:** Both *font* and *basefont* tags are now deprecated. Consequently, you may not use them. Instead we use CSS (**C**ascading **S**tyle **S**heets).

In this chapter we will use font and color with the font tag. In spite of the font tag being deprecated, you still need to know how the HTML websites use this tag. We will cover **CSS** in the next chapter.

The **BaseFont** tag keeps the entire text in the same font.
You may want to know some tags before using them.
The three attributes of the font are color, size and face.

<basefont> </basefont>	Keeping the same font for entire text
<font></font>	Change the font
<font size ="2"> </font>	Size of font =2 points
<font color="red">	Change color to red
<font face="Arial"> </font>	Uses family font = Arial

Example: 3.1

```
1.  <!DOCTYPE HTML PUBLIC "-//W3C//DTD HTML 4.01 Transitional//EN"
    "http://www.w3.org/TR/html4/loose.dtd">
2.  <head>
3.  <meta http-equiv="Content-Type" content="text/html; charset=iso-8859-1">
4.  <title>Basefont</title>
5.  </head>
6.  <body>  <div>
7.  <basefont size="4" color="blue">
8.  <p> Entire text will be in the same color and the same font</p>
9.  <p> the second paragraph has the same font and color as the first one!</p>
10. </div> </body>
11. </html>
```

The basefont remains the same throughout the entire text with the same size, color and face. We will later discuss the deprecation of the basefont. The word deprecation means disapproval by the company. In this case, both the font and basefont are **deprecated** by W3C.

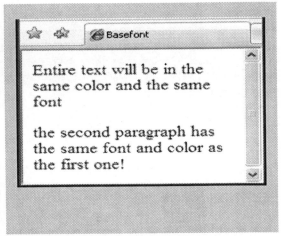

Now, try to add a line with a different font in the middle of the text. You will see that the middle text font is different and that the last line will remain the same as the *basefont* order. For example, we changed the middle line's font to 8.

```
<basefont size="4" color="blue">
<p> Entire text will be in the same color and the same font</p>
<font size ="8"> Different size</font>
<p> the second paragraph has the same font and color as the first one! </p>
```

Font attributes

We mentioned earlier that the <font> tag provides three attributes: color, size and face. Here you see all three used in one complete program. See this example.

Example: 3.2

1. <!DOCTYPE HTML PUBLIC "-//W3C//DTD HTML 4.01 Transitional//EN" "http://www.w3.org/TR/html4/loose.dtd">
2. <head>
3. <meta http-equiv="Content-Type" content="text/html; charset=iso-8859-1">
4. <title>Fonts</title>
5. </head>
6. <p><font size="5" color="blue" face="Verdana">No</font>
7. war is good war!</p>
8. <p><font size="2" color="red" face="san serif">All Wars are bad!</font>
9. </body>
10. </html>

The letter "No" is placed inside the font that is set to be 5 points in size. The rest are using the default font. The N is size 5, the color is blue and the face, which is the family font, is Verdana.

Now, try to close the font by the end of the paragraph and see the result.

The font continues to effects the text until you close the font with </font>. If you want to use a different font on the second paragraph then you need to set the new font.

```
<BODY>
<p><font size="5" color="blue"
face="Verdana">
No war is  good war!</font></p>
<p><font size="2" color="red"
face="san serif">All Wars are
bad!</font>
</BODY>
```

Big & small

The big tag tells the browser to print out the contents in a bigger than normal typeface. It is almost equivalent to <font size="+1" >
The small font tag forces the browser to print out almost equivalent to <font size="-1" >
Both tags need to be closed.

Example: 3.3
1. <!DOCTYPE HTML PUBLIC "-//W3C//DTD HTML 4.01 Transitional//EN" "http://www.w3.org/TR/html4/loose.dtd">
2. <head>
3. <meta http-equiv="Content-Type" content="text/html; charset=iso-8859-1">
4. <title>Big & Small</title>
5. </head>
6. <body>
7. <big> This is a big font.
</big>
8. <small> This is a small font.</small>
9. </body>
10. </html>

The big tag is a fixed font which is equivalent to **<Font size="+1">** and the small tag is equivalent to the **<font size="-1">**

You might be interested in making the text even smaller. If so, use the following double <small> tag:
<small> <small> This is a small font.**</small> </small>**

Colors

There are several ways to implement colors in HTML. One of the easiest ways is to use generic colors by using the name of the color. The generic colors usually exist in 16 basic colors and you simply need to call their names. For example, there is *blue*, *black*, *red*, etc. We can change the text color or background color.

Names of 16 basic colors that exist, and you can use them in HTML							
Aqua	Black	Blue	Fuchsia	Gray	Green	Lime	Maroon
Navy	Olive	Red	Purple	Silver	White	Teal	Yellow

Changing text colors

You can use a font color tag to change the color of the text. You have already seen them in this chapter.
<Font color="blue">

Example: 3.4
1. <!DOCTYPE HTML PUBLIC "-//W3C//DTD HTML 4.01 Transitional//EN" "http://www.w3.org/TR/html4/loose.dtd">
2. <head>
3. <meta http-equiv="Content-Type" content="text/html; charset=iso-8859-1">
4. <title>Text color</title>
5. </head>
6. <body>
7. <font color="blue">This is Blue
</font>
8. <font color="maroon">This is Maroon</font>
9. </body> </html>

RGB

Another way to work with HTML color is by using *RGB* values. RGB refers to the **R**ed, **G**reen and **B**lue base colors. By combining these three main colors in various ways, we can create many different colors. Each R, G and B has full levels of intensity ranging from 0 to 100%. Each is represented by decimal numbers 0 to 255, making 256 numbers. The total number of available colors is **256x256x256 = 16777216**. Yes, it provides more than *4 million* colors. HTML color code contains a six digit hexadecimal color format: the first pair is allocated to red, the second pair is allocated to green and the last pair is allocated to blue. In reality, however, many computer screens just can't handle all of these colors. There are differences in the various browsers. Yours might not be able to show some of your desired colors. However, today the capacity of browsers is enormous so it should not be a major problem. There are 216 colors which are called ***color safe***. PC and MAC both regard these colors in the same way.

RGB values

rgb(255 , 255 , 255)	White
rgb(255 , 0 , 0)	Red
rgb(0 , 255 , 0)	Green
rgb(0 , 0 , 255)	Blue
rgb(0, 0 , 0)	Black

Example: 3.5

1. `<!DOCTYPE HTML PUBLIC "-//W3C//DTD HTML 4.01 Transitional//EN" "http://www.w3.org/TR/html4/loose.dtd">`
2. `<head>`
3. `<meta http-equiv="Content-Type" content="text/html; charset=iso-8859-1">`
4. `<title>RGB</title>`
5. `</head>`
6. `<body>`
7. `<font color="rgb(138,43,226)"> RGB ->BlueViolet, BGB HEX->8A2BE2 <br></font>`
8. `<font color="rgb(100,149,237)"> RGB ->CornflowerBlue , BGB HEX -> 6495ED <br></font>`
9. `<font color="rgb(92,51,23)"> RGB ->baker's chocolate , BGB HEX -> 5C3317 <br></font>`
10. `<font color="rgb(128,128,0)"> RGB ->Olive , BGB HEX -> 808000 <br></font>`
11. `</body>`
12. `</html>`

In this example we use the RGB combination. You can use the equivalent value of hexadecimal.

In the next example we will use and implement the Hexadecimal values to generate the desired colors.

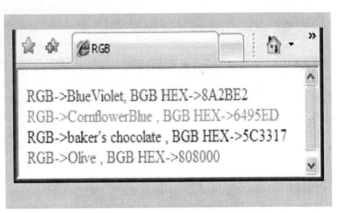

As mentioned, the Hexadecimal numbers format comes in 6 digits. It can look like this, #FFFFFF, it can be alphanumeric, #CC78CC, or it can take on a different form.

Decimal	0	1	2	3	4	5	6	7	8	9	10	11	12	13	14	15
Hexadecimal	0	1	2	3	4	5	6	7	8	9	A	B	C	D	E	F

The letter **F** is the maximum number which represents the white color: #FFFFFF.
To convert the hexadecimal to the decimal number, use the following formula.
(Letter * 16)+ Letter
Therefore **#FFFFFF** is (15 * 16) + 15=255 so the #FFFFFF is (255,255, 255)
Another example:
Convert **#DC143C** to decimal.
DC= (13 * 16) +12 =220
14= (1 *16) + 4=20
3C= (3*16) + 12=60
It becomes (220, 20, 60)

▮► **Note:** Any time the pair of three colors RGB are exactly the same, it provides a shaded color like rgb (100,100,100).

Example: 3.6

1. <!DOCTYPE HTML PUBLIC "-//W3C//DTD HTML 4.01 Transitional//EN" "http://www.w3.org/TR/html4/loose.dtd">
2. <head>
3. <meta http-equiv="Content-Type" content="text/html; charset=iso-8859-1">
4. <title>Hexadecimal color</title>
5. </head>
6. <body>
7. <font color="#DC143C"> What color is this?
</font>
8. <font color="#DC55CC"> So, What color is this?</font>
9. </body>
10. </html>

Bgcolor

The *bgcolor* attribute is used for the background of your page. The general form is <BODY bgcolor="Yellow"> Here the generic name is used. You can use a Hexadecimal such as <BODY bgcolor ="#CCFFCC">

Example: 3.7

1. <!DOCTYPE HTML PUBLIC "-//W3C//DTD HTML 4.01 Transitional//EN" "http://www.w3.org/TR/html4/loose.dtd">
2. <head>
3. <meta http-equiv="Content-Type" content="text/html; charset=iso-8859-1">
4. <title>Bgcolor </title>
5. </head>
6. <body bgcolor="black">
7. <FONT color="white" size="+2" face="Arial"> <b> White text with black background! </b></font>
8. </body>
9. </html>

The <BODY bgcolor="black"> tag makes the background of the webpage black. You can use any other color. Use the color's name from the *216 safe-color*. You can use the hexadecimal value. Here the background is in pure black and the text is in pure white.
The body tag must be closed by the end.

Review questions

1- List three attributes of font.
2- If you close the font tag on the first line, then the second line does not obey the font.   True   False
3- What is the difference between <font size="+1" > and <font size="1" >?
4- The Maroon color is one of the basic colors.   True   False
5- There are **16777216** fonts available. How do you get this large of a number?
6- What color does this RBG (255,255, 2555) generate?
7- What letter is the highest in the hexadecimal?
8- What color will print out if the three values of RBG are the same (for example, 90,90,90)?
9- How do you make the background blue?
10- Convert A2DDC5 hexadecimal into a decimal number.

Answers

1-Size, Color, Face
2-True
3- The <font size="+1" > is the same as <big>
4-True
5- 256x256x256
6- White
7-F
8- Shade
9- <BODY bgcolor="blue">
10-(162,221,197)

Chapter 4

Adding Styles to HTML

- Introduction
- Why CSS
- HTML head contents
- Font with CSS
- Font size
- Font family
- Multi font's family
- Font Style
- Font Variant
- Boldness
- Color
- Background-Color of Text
- Body background
- Review questions
- Answers

Introduction

So far we have been working with HTML, which is a very simple script to use. However, HTML has a somewhat limited capacity. We may need some other styles to add to the HTML. For example, the HTML colors and fonts are deprecated by **W3C**, so instead we must use the CSS (Cascading Style Sheet). The CSS is also easy to use and to understand. It provides pre-style design. When you use CSS along with HTML, you will see that the code becomes significantly short, making the browser implementation faster than regular or pure HTML. You can style your text and save it in a file with the **.css** extension, then call it in the head of a HTML file. In this chapter we will look at many relevant examples in order to learn the CSS in a simple and efficient way. We will discuss the CSS completely in the second part of this book.

Why CSS?

Some parts of the HTML have been deprecated, meaning that the W3C recommends that we don't use them in the future. We should use CSS instead. The most important tags like <Basefont>, <font> and its attributes (color, size and face), will no longer be available in the near future. In this chapter we must use some features of CSS to replace the HTML fonts tag. You will learn CSS in more detail in the proceeding chapters.

HTML head contents

Previously we explained that the HTML *head* contains *title*, *Meta* tags and *script*. Now we add another two methods, **style** and **link**, to the head.

Once again, try to look at the common head contents in HTML.

Common HTML head contents

```
1.  <HEAD>
2.  <title> Rabbits for sale</title>

3.  <meta http-equiv="Content-Type" content="text/html; charset =iso-8859-1">

4.  <meta name="keywords" content="Black rabbits, White rabbits, Maroon
    rabbits">

5.  <meta name="description" content="Our rabbits are playing in garden.">

6.  <script type="text/javascript">
7.  </script>

8.  <link href="Rab.css" rel="stylesheet" type="text/css" />

9.  <style type="text/css">
10. <!--
11. .style1 {
12. color: #CC0000;
13. font-weight: bold;
14. }
15. .style2 {font-weight: bold}
16. -->
17. </style>
    </HEAD>
```

Analysis: The head begins in line 1 and it ends in the last line. Line 2 is the title which will be shown on the title-bar of your browser. Line 3 is the Meta *CHARSET* which defines the language. On line 4, the Meta tag is placed to declare the keywords. The keywords are the words you choose to describe your page and which will be used by search engines to find your page. For example, if someone types *white rabbit* in the Google search engine, your site will be shown. Line 5 is the description of the page. This will be shown in the part of the search engine which describes what your site is about. The script tag is placed on lines 6 and 7 to invoke the JavaScript and to indicate that this site uses JavaScript. On line 8, you will see the link which loads the file name with the css extension, and you will see the **CSS** code indicating the usability of the style Sheet into HTML code on lines 9 to 16.

Font with CSS

Now we will try to use simple fonts with the help of CSS. The CSS allows us to manipulate the text more efficiently. We can create a style and place it into the HTML head. Then we can apply it throughout the entire text. This is the general declaration of style sheets:

Selector {property: value;}
H1 {font-size:30px; } So *H1* is the selector, font-size: is a property and 30px is a value.
Just type and run this Basic HTML script:
Save your file as any name.html

Example: 4.1
1.   <HTML>
2.   <HEAD>
3.   <TITLE>Just HTML</TITLE>
4.   </HEAD>
5.   <BODY>
6.   Stylesheets: solves HTML 4.0 problems
7.   We call selector <u>B</u> to generate 24-Pixle
8.   </BODY>
9.   </HTML>

This is just a simple HTML. It produces the result you see. There is no specified font. It simply outputs what has been set within the script code.

Now, just paste this code inside the HTML head, call it in the body of program, and then look at the result.

Save the above file as **anyname.html**

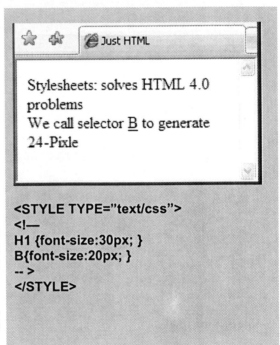

```
<STYLE TYPE="text/css">
<!—
H1 {font-size:30px; }
B{font-size:20px; }
-- >
</STYLE>
```

Example: 4.2

1. <!DOCTYPE HTML PUBLIC "-//W3C//DTD HTML 4.01//EN"
2. "http://www.w3.org/TR/html4/Strict.dtd">
3. <head>
4. <title>Style Sheets</title>
5. <meta http-equiv="Content-Type" content="text/html; charset=iso-8859-1">
6. **<STYLE TYPE="text/css">**
7. **H1** {font-size:30px; }
8. **B**{font-size:20px; }
9. **</STYLE>**
10. </head> <BODY>
11. <H1>Stylesheets: solves HTML 4.0 problems</H1>
12. <p><B>We call the [B] selector to generate 20-Pixle font</B></p>
13. </BODY> </HTML>

> # Stylesheets: solves HTML 4.0 problems
>
> **We call the [B] selector to generate 20-Pixle font**

▮► **Note:** There must not be white space between property and value. *Font-size* is a property,30px is a value

Analysis: The above style-sheets are called **type style**. This is because we use the H1 and the B, both of which are HTML types (understood by HTML code). Look at the inside of the body of the program. Line 11, called <H1>, corresponds to line 7 from the head which is set to 30 pixels. Line 12, the B, corresponds to line 8 from the head.

▮► **Note:** We must first create styles inside the head and then call them inside the body of our program. Anywhere we can call **H1**, either only once or many times, a font size of 30 pixels is generated.

All styles must be placed within the HTML head:

```
<HEAD>
<TITLE>Style Sheets</TITLE>
<STYLE TYPE="text/css">
H1 {font-size:30px; }
B{font-size:20px; }
</STYLE>
</HEAD>
```

Font size

There are many attributes that generate font size in CSS. Below are some attributes that are more helpful. You can use them within your HTML code.

Font-size can be chosen from one of these groups:

- <absolute-size>
- <relative-size>
- <percentage>

CSS Font size groups			
Length group	Absolute group	Relative group	Percentage group
font-size: normal font-size:10px font-size:12pt	font-size:x-small font-size:xx-small font-size:small font-size:medium font-size:large font-size:x-large font-size:xx-large	font-size:smaller font-size:larger	font-size:50%

pt (points; 1pt=1/72in)
pc (picas; 1pc=12pt)
em (the height of the element's font)
px (pixels)
Please note, "pt" is a print unit, and not an exact screen unit.
Fonts can be manipulated by these features: font-size, font-style, font-variant, font-weight, line-height and font-family.

Example: 4.3
1.   <!DOCTYPE HTML PUBLIC "-//W3C//DTD HTML 4.01//EN"
2.   "http://www.w3.org/TR/html4/Strict.dtd">
3.   <head> <title>Different Style Sheets</title>
4.   <meta http-equiv="Content-Type" content="text/html; charset=iso-8859-1">
5.   <STYLE TYPE="text/css">
6.   H1 {font-size:20pt; }
7.   H2 {font-size:20px; }
8.   H3 {font-size:100%;}
9.   H4 {font-size:150%;}
10. </STYLE> <BODY>
11. <H1>This size is 20 point</H1>
12. <H2>This size is 20 pixel</H2>
13. <H3>This size is 100%</H3>
14. <H4>This size is 150%</H4>
15. </BODY>
16. </HTML>

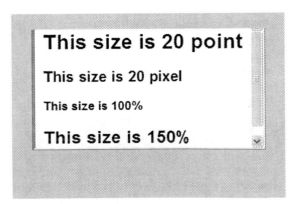

Font family

The font family defines the font name by the available fonts in your system. Sometimes it is difficult to know which browser clients are using. The differences between Mac and PC can also cause a problem. You must use the family font in order to generate exact or closely related fonts.

Example: 4.4

```
1. <!DOCTYPE HTML PUBLIC "-//W3C//DTD HTML 4.01//EN"
2. "http://www.w3.org/TR/html4/Strict.dtd">
3. <head>
4. <title>Font Family</title>
5. <meta http-equiv="Content-Type" content="text/html; charset=iso-8859-1">
6. <style type="text/css">
7. h1 {font-size:16pt; font-family: times;}
8. h2{font-size:18pt; font-family: forte;}
9. </style>
10.</head>
11.<body>
12.<h1>
13.Text with a times font 16pt.
14.</h1>
15.<H2>
16.Text with a forte font 18pt.
17.</H2>
18.<p>Text with no specified font.</p>
19.</body>
20.</html>
```

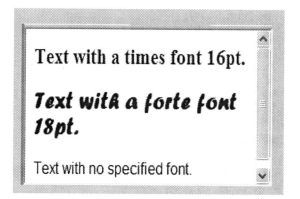

The family font that we use here (time, forte) both exist inside our computer, Therefore it doesn't cause any problems.

What happens if the font is not provided by your native system (your computer)?

In this case it automatically returns to the default font, *times new roman*.

In the same example we will change the font to a font-name that does not exist. For example instead of **forte**, we will use **fortes**.

```
<style type="text/css">
h1{font-size:16pt;font-family: times;}
h2{font-size:18pt;font-family: fortes;}
</style>
```

You see here that the *fortes* font returns to the default font, simply because the fortes font does not exist.

We can use multi-family fonts to solve this font problem

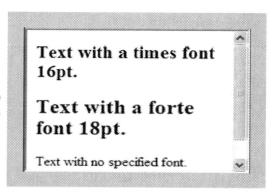

Multi-fonts family

We can use multi-fonts in CSS. Multi-fonts allow us to use different fonts. If the first font is not available then it checks for the second one, and so on.

Example: 4.5

1. <!DOCTYPE HTML PUBLIC "-//W3C//DTD HTML 4.01//EN"
2. "http://www.w3.org/TR/html4/Strict.dtd">
3. <head>
4. <title>Default Font </title>
5. <meta http-equiv="Content-Type" content="text/html; charset=iso-8859-1">
6. <style type="text/css">
7. H1{font-family: fox, "Courier new", sans-serif;}
8. </style> </head> <body>
9. <h1>
10. What is this font?
11. </h1>
12. <p>
13. Text with no specified font.
14. </p>
15. </body>
16. </html>

```
H1
{
font-family: fox, "Courier new", sans-serif;
}
```
We use several fonts in this example. The first font, Fox, is not available. It must, therefore, check for the second font. If the second font is not available then it will check for the third one, and will continue in this way until an available font is found. In this case the second font, **Courier new**, is available, so it can output the second family font.

▐▶ **Note:** If the font's name contains more than one word, use the double string. For example, Courier New comprises of two words. We have to put them inside the string: **"Courier new"**.

Font Style

CSS font-style contains these styles
- **font-style:normal**
- **font-style:italic**
- **font-style:oblique**

Example: 4.6
1. <!DOCTYPE HTML PUBLIC "-//W3C//DTD HTML 4.01//EN"
2. "http://www.w3.org/TR/html4/Strict.dtd">
3. <head>
4. <title> Font Styles </title>
5. <meta http-equiv="Content-Type" content="text/html; charset=iso-8859-1">
6. <style type="text/css">
7. h1 {font-style: italic}
8. h2 {font-style: normal}
9. h3 {font-style: oblique}
10. </style>
11. </head>
12. <body>
13. <h1>Italic style</h1>
14. <h2>Normal style</h2>
15. <h3>Oblique style</h3>
16. </body>
17. </html>

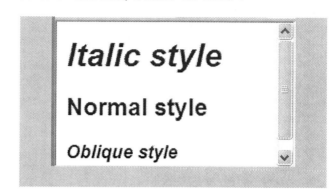

Font Variant

The font variant property is designed to display fonts in **small-caps** or in a **normal** font.

Example: 4.7
1. <!DOCTYPE HTML PUBLIC "-//W3C//DTD HTML 4.01//EN"
2. "http://www.w3.org/TR/html4/Strict.dtd">
3. <head> <title> Font Variant </title>
4. <meta http-equiv="Content-Type" content="text/html; charset=iso-8859-1">
5. <style type="text/css">
6. P {font-variant: normal}
7. I {font-variant: small-caps}
8. </style> </head> <body>
9. <P> This is a normal font.</P>
10. <div>
11. <I> This is a small-caps font.</I>
12. </div>
13. <h5>This has no variant.</h5>
14. </body>
15. </html>

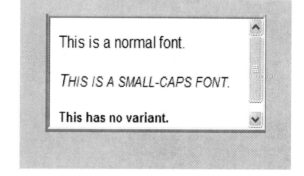

Boldness

You can use **font-weight** instead of bold. It is still a bold style but has more control in the size (from100-900).
p.Nor {font-weight: normal}
p.Bol {font-weight: bold}
p.Gro {font-weight: 800}

In this example we use class to call our "P". We use the P for full access to the dot notation: **P.Something**. We use class in order to invoke the CSS features <p class="Nor">.

Example: 4.8
1. <!DOCTYPE HTML PUBLIC "-//W3C//DTD HTML 4.01//EN"
2. "http://www.w3.org/TR/html4/Strict.dtd">
3. <head> <title> Boldness Font </title>
4. <meta http-equiv="Content-Type" content="text/html; charset=iso-8859-1">
5. <style type="text/css">
6. p.Nor {font-weight: normal}
7. p.Bol {font-weight: bold}
8. p.Gro {font-weight: 800}
9. </style> </head> <body>
10. <p class="Nor">
11. This is a normal font.
12. </p>
13. <p class="Bol">   This is in bold.
14. </p>
15. <p class="Gro">   This is in Gross font 800.
16. </p> </body>
17. </html>

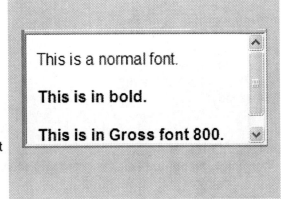

Colors
The text color is the same as the font in CSS. Use ***color:red***, and so on. It is very simple. Just look at this example.

Example: 4.9
1. <html> <head>
2. <Title> Color </Title>
3. <style type="text/css">
4. p { font-size:15pt; color: blue; }
5. </style> </head>
6. <body> <p> Nice blue text!</p>
7. </body> </html>

Background-Color of Text
Use *background-color:yellow;* to invoke the background of the text:
p { font-size:15pt; Background-color:yellow;color: blue; }

Example: 4.10
1. `<!DOCTYPE HTML PUBLIC "-//W3C//DTD HTML 4.01//EN"`
2. `"http://www.w3.org/TR/html4/Strict.dtd">`
3. `<head>`
4. `<title> Color </title>`
5. `<meta http-equiv="Content-Type" content="text/html; charset=iso-8859-1">`
6. `<style type="text/css">`
7. `p { font-size:15pt;  Background-color:yellow;color: blue; }`
8. `</style>`
9. `</head>`
10. `<body>`
11. `<p>` Nice blue text in yellow `background!</p>`
12. `</body>`
13. `</html>`

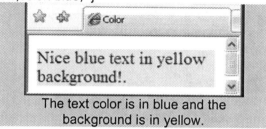

The text color is in blue and the
background is in yellow.

Body background

Use the **body** instead of the **P**. Then invoke the body to set the webpage background to the desired color.

Example: 4.11
1. `<!DOCTYPE HTML PUBLIC "-//W3C//DTD HTML 4.01//EN"`
2. `"http://www.w3.org/TR/html4/Strict.dtd">`
3. `<head>`
4. `<title> Color </title>`
5. `<meta http-equiv="Content-Type" content="text/html; charset=iso-8859-1">`
6. `<style type="text/css">`
7. `body { font-size:15pt;  Background-color : yellow; color : blue; }`
8. `</style>`
9. `</head>`
10. `<body>`
11. `<p>`
12. Nice blue text in yellow background!
13. `</p>`
14. `</body>`
15. `</html>`

Review questions

1- Why should we use CSS in HTML?
2- List five common features in HTML that must be placed inside the head.
3- Give the general syntax of font decorating.
4- What is difference between 14pt and 14px?
5- You should not leave space between property and value in CSS. True False
6- What is the font-family?
7- List two font variants.
8- List three font styles.
9- How do you declare text color?
10- How do you declare page background?

Answers

1- Some parts of HTML like the font, color, U and I are deprecated by W3C. Therefore, we must use CSS features which give us more flexibility to program our client webpage.
2- Title, Charset, CSS style, JavaScript and Link
3- Selector{property:value;}
4- 14pt means 14 point pt (points; 1pt=1/72in) for printer
    14px means pixels.
5- True
6- Different font types that exist in your computer and can be shown by the browser.
7- Normal, Small-Caps
8- Italic, normal, oblique
9- *color:red*
10- Background-color: yellow

Chapter 5

Working with tables

Introduction

The HTML table has been an integral part of web design for a long time. It is easy to create a table and manipulate its rows and columns. It is used for the layout design of very basic web pages. The border, height, width and many other attributes give the HTML table great abilities to create a tabular format. In fact, the table is not only used to create a layout. It also has a large application, especially when we cover the database system. In simple terms, all elements of the database are saved in a table. We have to create a table to load and retrieve the data in a nice tabular format, using relevant colors and fonts. Usually we use a table with these features: Tabular format, Databases, HTML form, layout, adjustment, and shopping card, among others. In this chapter we will work on several aspects of the HTML table.

Basic tables

The table is one the most useful elements in web design. Rarely can you see a webpage that does not use some form of tables. Tables allow the data to be organized.
First look at these tags:

<TABLE> Generates a table.
<TR> Generates table row.
<TD> Generates Table Column, TD stands for "Table Data" sometimes called data cell, the data will be placed into TD.
<TH> Generates Table Header.
Each tag must be closed in an appropriate place like:
<TR>
<TD> Data **</TD>**
</TR>
Look at this simple table 2 X 2 (2 Rows by 2 Columns) called **2 by 2**.

OOPS, where is the table? The above output is not in the tabular format. Did you forget to use a border?
                Oh, yes

Example: 5.1
1. <!DOCTYPE HTML PUBLIC "-//W3C//DTD HTML 4.01//EN"
2. "http://www.w3.org/TR/html4/Strict.dtd">
3. <Head>
4. <Title>Basic table</title>
5. **<meta   http-equiv   =   "Content-Type" content = "text/html; charset=iso-8859-1">**
6. </head> <body> <TABLE>
7. <TR>
8. <TD>Milk</TD> <TD>$2.99</TD>
9. </TR>
10. <TR>
11. <TD>Bananas</TD> <TD>$2.49</TD>
12. </TR> </TABLE> </body>
13. </HTML>

The character **encoding** tells browser what type of character has to be encoded. On line 5 we use the character encoding.

  <meta http-equiv = "Content-Type" content = "text/html; charset=iso-8859-1">

Table Border

Setting a border is necessary for table visibility. The above example generates a table but the border is not visible on your browser.
Now we will set a border for the table. On the table tag, use border=1 like this:
<Table border="1">

Example: 5.2
1. <!DOCTYPE HTML PUBLIC "-//W3C// DTD HTML 4.01//EN"
2. "http://www.w3.org/TR/html4/Strict.dtd">
3. <Head>
4. <Title>Table with simple border</title>
5. <meta http-equiv="Content-Type" content ="text/html; charset=iso-8859-1">
6. </head> <body>
7. <TABLE border="1">
8. <TR>
9. <TD>Milk</TD> <TD>$2.99</TD>
10. </TR>
11. <TR>
12. <TD>Banana</TD> <TD>$2.49</TD>
13. </TR>
14. </TABLE> </body>
15. </HTML>

The border gives some thickness to the table. Now if you set **border="8"** you see that the table becomes thicker.
<TABLE border="8">

Table header

The header gives more clarity to the table. Each column must have a header which indicates the column's name. Here you will see a table with name, age and balance. By default the header is in bold.

Example: 5.3
1. <!DOCTYPE HTML PUBLIC "-//W3C// DTD HTML 4.01//EN"
2. "http://www.w3.org/TR/html4/Strict.dtd">
3. <Head>
4. <Title>Table header</title>
5. <meta http-equiv="Content-Type" content ="text/html; charset=iso-8859-1">
6. </head> <body>
7. <TABLE border="2">
8. <TR> <TH>Name</TH>
9. <TH>Age</TH>
10. <TH>Balance</TH>
11. </TR> <TR>
12. <TD>Gormeh</TD> <TD>Sabzi</TD><TD>$12.95 </TD> </TR> <TR>
13. <TD>Alam</TD> <TD>Shangi</TD><TD>$125.25 </TD> </TR> <TR>
14. <TD>Peter</TD> <TD>Hansen</TD><TD>$120.95 </TD>
15. </TR> </TABLE>
16. </body>
17. </HTML>

Name	Age	Balance
Gormeh	Sabzi	$12.95
Alam	Shangi	$125.25
Peter	Hansen	$120.95

Spanning rows

The HTML table must be modified according to different situations. You might want to have a bigger cell on the left side of the table. To do this you would use the **ROWSPAN** attribute. The *ROWSPAN* simply eliminates the indicated rows:

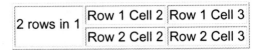

2 rows in 1	Row 1 Cell 2	Row 1 Cell 3
	Row 2 Cell 2	Row 2 Cell 3

Example: 5.4
```
<!DOCTYPE HTML PUBLIC "-//W3C//DTD HTML
4.01//EN"
"http://www.w3.org/TR/html4/Strict.dtd">
 <Head>
<Title>Row Span</title>
<meta                     http-equiv="Content-Type"
content="text/html; charset=iso-8859-1">
</head>
  <body>
  <table border="1">
  <tr><td rowspan="2">Elephant</td>
  <td>Cat</td><td>Dog</td></tr>
  <tr><td>Rat</td><td>Rabbit</td></tr>
  </table></body></HTML>
```

We designed a bigger space for elephant (the big guy) and small spaces for the rest.

You can use <TH> to create a header or title for each cell.

Example: 5.5
1. <!DOCTYPE HTML PUBLIC "-//W3C//DTD HTML 4.01//EN"
2. "http://www.w3.org/TR/html4/Strict.dtd">
3. <Head>
4. <Title>Header</title>
5. <meta http-equiv="Content-Type" content="text/html; charset=iso-8859-1">
6. </head> <body>
7. <table border="1"> <tr>

8. <th>Big</th>
9. <th>Small</th>
10. <th>Medium</th>
11. <tr><td rowspan="2">Elephant</td>
12. <td>Cat</td><td>Dog</td></tr>
13. <tr><td>Rat</td><td>Rabbit</td></tr>
14. </table></body>
15. </HTML>

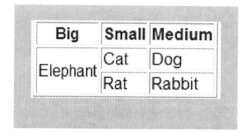

Spanning columns

COLSPAN is a way to eliminate several columns from your table. Look at this example to see how COLSPAN works.

Example: 5.6
1. <!DOCTYPE HTML PUBLIC "-//W3C//DTD HTML 4.01//EN"
2. "http://www.w3.org/TR/html4/Strict.dtd">
3. <Head>
4. <Title>Column Span</title>
5. <meta http-equiv="Content-Type" content="text/html; charset=iso-8859-1">
6. </Head>
7. <body> <table border="1">
8. <tr>
9. <td Colspan="2"> Shopping card for online bookstore</td>
10. </tr> <tr> <td>HTML BOOK</td><td>$22.95</td></tr>
11. <tr><td>Total Amount</td><td>$22.95</td></tr>
12. <tr><td colspan="2">There will no tax on the selected item</td></tr>
13. </table> </body>
14. </HTML>

Shopping card for online bookstore	
HTML BOOK	$22.95
Total Amount	$22.95
There will no tax on the selected item	

▍▶ **Note:** COLSPAN means how many horizontal and ROWSPAN means how many vertical. We have seen the COLSPAN and the ROWSPAN. Now look at how both are combined in the same program.

Example: 5.7
```
1.  <!DOCTYPE HTML PUBLIC "-//W3C//DTD HTML 4.01//EN"
2.  "http://www.w3.org/TR/html4/Strict.dtd">
3.  <Head>
4.  <Title>Row and Col Span</title>
5.  <meta http-equiv="Content-Type" content="text/html; charset=iso-8859-1">
6.  </head>
7.  <body> <table border="1">
8.  <tr>
9.  <td Colspan="3"> Admission and Registrar office </td>
10. </tr>
11. <tr><td rowspan="2">Student <br>name</td>
12. <td>Programming</td><td>95%</td></tr>
13. <tr><td>Math</td><td>86%</td></tr>
14. <tr><td colspan="3">Note: mark less than 50% is fail
15. </td></tr>
16. </table> </body>
17. </HTML>
```

Admission and Registrar office		
Student name	Programming	95%
	Math	86%
Note: mark less than 50% is fail		

Cell padding & Cell spacing

CELLSPACING controls spaces the between the cells. The space value is 2 by default. CELLPADDING controls the amount of space between text (content of cell) and the border (wall of cell). It is 1 by default.

Example: 5.8
```
1.  <html> <head>
2.  <Title> Cell padding</Title>
3.  </head> <body>
4.  <h3>Without cellpadding</h3>
5.  <table border="1">
6.  <tr>
7.  <th>First Name</th>
8.  <th>Last Name</th>
16. <h3>With cellpadding</h3>
17. <table border="1"cellpadding="12">
18. <tr> <th>First Name</th>
19. <th>Last Name</th>
20. <tr> <tr>
21. <td>Car</td>
22. <td>Wash</td>
```

9.   <tr>
10. <td>Car</td>
11. <td>Wash</td>
12. </tr> <tr>
13. <td>Web</td>
14. <td>Design</td>
15. </tr> </table>

23. </tr> <tr>
24. <td>Web</td>
25. <td>Design</td>
26. </tr> </table> </body>
27. </html>

As you can see on the first table, the cellpadding attribute is not set, therefore each word like "Car, Wash" is displayed very close to the wall of the table.

On the second table we set the cellpadding attribute to 12, therefore it displays a little further away from the table wall.

Without cellpadding

First Name	Last Name
Car	Wash
Web	Design

With cellpadding

First Name	Last Name
Car	Wash
Web	Design

Cellspacing

The Cellspacing attribute makes space between the cells. Look at this example's output to see the space between cells.

Example: 5.9

1.   <html> <head>
2.   <Title> Cell Spacing</Title>
3.   </head> <body>
4.   <h3>Without cellSpacing</h3>
5.   <table border="1">
6.   <tr> <th>First Name</th>
7.   <th>Last Name</th>
8.   </tr> <tr>
9.   <td>Car</td>
10. <td>Wash</td>
11. </tr> <tr>
12. <td>Web</td>
13. <td>Design</td>
14. </tr> </table>
15. <h3>With cellSpacing</h3>

16. <table border="5"cellspacing="12">
17. <tr>
18. <th>First Name</th>
19. <th>Last Name</th>
20. </tr> <tr>
21. <td>Car</td>
22. <td>Wash</td>
23. </tr> <tr>
24. <td>Web</td>
25. <td>Design</td>
26. </tr> </table> </body>
27. </html>

No cellspacing is designed on the first table. Everything is shown in the default view.

On the second table, we make the border a little thicker in order to be visible. The spacing is "12". Consequently, you see that the cells are not attached to each other. We remove the cellpadding so that the content of the cells is displayed on the edge of the table border.

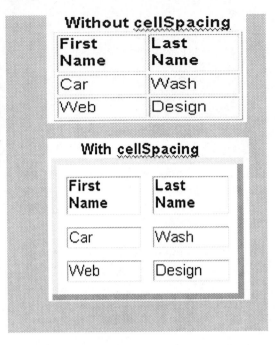

Table alignment

Alignment helps us to position the table or content of the table correctly. There are two types of alignments: **VALIGN** is used for vertical alignments and the **ALIGN** is used for horizontal alignments.

Align can be use for **Left, Right, and Center**.

Valign can be used for **Top**, **Middle** and **Bottom**. For example, VALIGN="TOP" or VALIGN ="BOTTOM".

The horizontal default alignment for contents of TD is *left* and the vertical default is *middle*.

In this example we show the three different alignments.

▮▶ **Note:** By default table will be aligned to the left.

Example: 5.10

```
1.  <!DOCTYPE HTML PUBLIC "-//W3C//DTD HTML 4.01 Transitional//EN"
       "http://www.w3.org/TR/html4/loose.dtd">
2.  <head>
3.  <Title>Table Alignment</title>
4.  <meta http-equiv="Content-Type" content="text/html; charset=iso-8859-1">
5.  </head>
6.  <body> <table align="left" border="1">
7.  <tr><th colspan="2"> Table shifted left</th></tr>
8.  <tr><td> Left</td><td>Hand</td></tr>
9.  <tr><td> Turn</td><td>Left</td></tr>
```

10. </table>

11. <table align="center" border="1">
12. <tr><th colspan="2"> Table in center</th></tr>
13. <tr><td> Center</td><td>Page</td></tr>
14. <tr><td> Middle</td><td>Side</td></tr>
15. </table>

 <table align="right" border="1" >
16. <tr><th colspan="2"> Table shifted right</th></tr>
17. <tr><td> Right</td><td>Hand</td></tr>
18. <tr><td> Turn</td><td>Right</td></tr>
19. </table> </body>
20. </html>

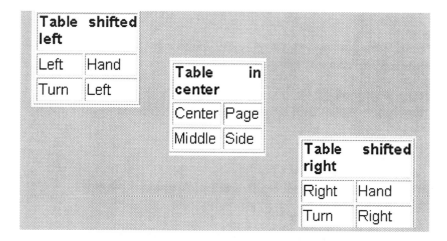

Table color

The background of the table can be in any desired color. We can also put each cell in a different color. We use **BGCOLOR** in order to make the background of our table. Look at the following example to see the color-background.

Example: 5.11
1. <!DOCTYPE HTML PUBLIC "-//W3C//DTD HTML 4.01 **Transitional**//EN"
    "http://www.w3.org/TR/html4/loose.dtd">
2. <head> <Title>HTML Comments</title>
3. <meta http-equiv="Content-Type" content="text/html; charset=iso-8859-1">
4. </head>
5. <body>
6. <TABLE BORDER="3" bgcolor ="#f0e68c">
7. <TR> <TD>This is the Khaki background </TD> </TR> <TR>
8. <TD> Khaki background is nice </TD>
9. </TR> </TABLE> </body>
10. </html>

This is the Khaki background

Khaki background is nice

The whole background is turned to Khaki color. Now we will try to set the background of each cell in a different color. In this case, the attribute of <TD> must be in a color such as <TD bgcolor="#xxxx">

Remember: *bgcolor* attribute is deprecated, means can not be used by HTML anymore therefore we must use CSS Style Sheet. Here we use inline CSS format. Check out this example.

Example: 5.12

```
 1. <!DOCTYPE HTML PUBLIC "-//W3C//DTD HTML 4.01//EN"
 2. "http://www.w3.org/TR/html4/Strict.dtd">
 3. <head>
 4. <Title>BGCOLOR</title>
 5. <meta http-equiv="Content-Type" content="text/html; charset=iso-8859-1">
 6. </head>
 7. <body>
 8. <TABLE BORDER="2">
 9. <TR>   <TD >
10. <p style="background: blue; color: yellow; font-size: 14pt;">
11. Light blue Cell </p> </TD>
12. <TD >
13. <p style="background: blue; color: yellow; font-size: 14pt;">
14. Golden color Cell </p> </TD>
15. </TR> </TABLE>   </body>
16. </html>
```

Light blue Cell Golden color Cell

In the table above, you see that the text colors and cell background colors are different. We use CSS for text color instead of <FONT COLOR> which is deprecated. You have seen CSS in the previous chapter.

▶ **Note:** If you want to set the color for the entire table, then set the different color for the table cell because the color will be over print. This means that the cell color will take over.

Table dimension

The width and height of the table can be set along with the table declaration.   For example,

<TABLE BORDER="2" width = 350 height = 100>

This adjusts the table size to 350 pixels in width and 100 pixels in height.

▐▶ **Note:** You may want to set the size of the table by a percentage, such as WIDTH= 75%, but not all browsers can handle that.

Example: 5.13

```
1.  <!DOCTYPE HTML PUBLIC "-//W3C//DTD HTML 4.01//EN"
2.  "http://www.w3.org/TR/html4/Strict.dtd">
3.  <head>
4.  <Title>Table Size</title>
5.  <meta http-equiv="Content-Type" content="text/html; charset=iso-8859-1">
6.  </head>
7.  <body>
8.  <TABLE BORDER="2" width="30%">
9.  <TR><TH>Centigrade</TH><TH> Fahrenheit </TH>
10. </TR> <TR> <TD> 15</TD><TD> 59</TD>
11. </TR> <TR> <TD> 20</TD><TD> 68</TD>
12. </TR> </TABLE> </body>
13. </html>
```

Centigrade	Fahrenheit
15	59
20	68

How about the width of a cell?
You can use <TD width="100">.

Caption

The descriptive of a table is called the caption. By default, the caption displays on the **top** of the table. But you can change this to be shown on the bottom of the table. You can also use align attributes along with the caption tag.

Example: 5.14

```
1.  <!DOCTYPE HTML PUBLIC "-//W3C//DTD HTML 4.01//EN"
2.  "http://www.w3.org/TR/html4/Transtional.dtd">
3.  <head>
4.  <Title>Caption</title>
5.  <meta http-equiv="Content-Type" content="text/html; charset=iso-8859-1">
6.  </head>
7.  <body>
8.  <TABLE BORDER="2">
```

9. <CAPTION>March Figure</CAPTION>
10. <TR>
11. <TD>Sales</TD><TD>$12000</TD>
12. </TR> <TR>
13. <TD>Expenses</TD> <TD>$4000</TD>
14. </TR> </TABLE> </body>
15. </html>

March Figure

Sales	$12000
Expenses	$4000

Now just change the caption on line 7 to
<CAPTION align="bottom">March
Figure</CAPTION>

You will see that it produces a bottom caption.

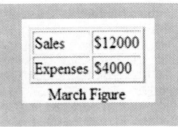

Review questions

1-What is the difference between <td> and <th>?

2-<tr> <td>**</td><td>**</td></tr> This creates two rows.   True   False

3- How do you declare a border for the Table?

4-<Table> tag needs a close tag</Table>   True   False

5-Colspan removes columns.   True   False

6-Rowspan removes rows.   True   False

7-How do you display a table on the right side of the webpage?

8-How do you make a table border thicker?

9-A table is aligned to the right of the page by default.   True   False

10-How do you create a table without a border?

Answers

1-The <th> is use for the header, by default it turns bold, the <td> is used to create a column.

2- False

3-<table border="1">

4-True

5-True

6-True

7-<table align="right">

8-<table border="X"> where the X is any number

9-False

10-<table border="0">

Chapter 6

Entities and Links

Introduction

The HTML entity allows us to deal with some of the problems found with browsers. Some browsers may not be able to parse some characters correctly. In the case of the greater than ">", for example, we must use the value of the" greater than" sign rather than its exact sign. HTML provides many entities which you can consult in the table of entities. Another sophisticated feature of HTML is its ability to link to the file, or to the ID, which has been previously set. In this chapter we will discuss both entities and the link.

How to use an entity

What are the HTML entities? The HTML entities are used when the browser cannot encode some characters, or when you can't enter the character through your keyboard, like the *euro* sign € or sign ≥ (some keyboards do not have the € character, for example). In HTML you can use spaces as you want but the browser generates only one space unless you use ** ** (No Break space). In fact, the HTML itself uses entities with the symbols < >, as with tags. Because of this, the browser may get confused with HTML tags and we must use entities for certain characters instead.

▮▶ **Note:** The entity in HTML is case sensitive. **rArr** is not the same as **rarr**.

Example: 6.1
1. <!DOCTYPE HTML PUBLIC "-//W3C//DTD HTML 4.01//EN"
2. "http://www.w3.org/TR/html4/Strict.dtd">
3. <head>
4. <title>Entities</title>
5. <meta http-equiv="Content-Type" content="text/html; charset=iso-8859-1">
6. </head> <body> <p>
7. ♦ 500 € = $750
8. ♦ H2 + O → H2O
9. ♦   What is the ≥ sign?
10. </p>   </body>
11. </HTML>

- 500 € = $750
- H2 + O → H2O
- What is the ≥ sign?

Analysis: Line 6 generates a diamond sign (♦) and we use ** ** which generates a   space. If you use two or three , then it generates 2 or 3 spaces(character spaces). Line 7 generates an arrow (right arrow) and line 8 generates the " ≥ "sign.

▶ **Note:** An entity has three parts:
Ampersand **&**
Name or number
Semi-colon;
Like: **&** *nbsp* **;**

You can use some special characters with the help of an HTML entity. Just look at this example.

Example: 6.2
1. <!DOCTYPE HTML PUBLIC "-//W3C//DTD HTML 4.01//EN"
2. "http://www.w3.org/TR/html4/Strict.dtd">
3. <head>
4. <title>Special Characters</title>
5. <meta http-equiv="Content-Type" content="text/html; charset=iso-8859-1">
6. </head>
7. <body> <p>
8. This book is copyright protected ©
9. Price: $29 and 25 ¢
10. </p>   </body>
11. </HTML>

This book is copyright protected ©
Price: $29 and 25 ¢

Here are some useful HTML entities. For a complete list of HTML entities, you can look at *HTML entities* via the Internet.

HTML Entities			
Character	Entity	Decimal	Result
quotation mark	&quot;	&#34;	"
ampersand	&amp;	&#38;	&
less-than sign	&lt;	&#60;	<
greater-than sign	&gt;	&#62;	>
euro sign	&euro;	&#8364;	€
copyright sign	&copy;	&#169;	©

Onload and onunload

When the page is finished loading, the result of **onload** will popup on the screen.

<Body onLoad="alert ('page is loaded')">

When the user leaves the page, the **onunload** shows up.

Now try to click on the close button on the browser. You will see the *onunload* message

Example: 6.3
1. <!DOCTYPE HTML PUBLIC "-//W3C// DTD HTML 4.01//EN"
2. "http://www.w3.org/TR/html4/Strict.dtd">
3. <head>
4. <title>ONLOAD</title>
5. <meta http-equiv="Content-Type" content="text/html; charset=iso-8859-1">
6. </head>
7. <body onload = "alert('Site is loaded')" onunload = "alert('Leaving the site')" >
8. <h1> Click on close button on browser!</h1>
9. </body> </HTML>

You will see that the when the page is finished loading, the message of **onload**, "*Site is loaded*", pops up. If you try to close the browser you will see the second message of **onunload**. This indicates that "*leaving the site*" is showing up.

Links

The link in HTML means several different linkages. One of the most useable links is the page link. Sometimes you have a large document with multiple headlines for which you will need to create some brief linkages. For example, your document contains 10 headlines and each headline contains one or more pages. In this case, you can simply create a clickable button which will automatically search and show the exact headline. Linkage can be an image, different pages, or different files. If you have a large document, you can create a clickable text like "Go to Top" at the end of the document in order to direct the document to the top of the page.

Example: 6.4
For this example you may need to download some large texts from the Internet.

```
<HTML>
<head>
<title>Linkage</title>
</head>
<body>
<pre>
<A Name="top"></A> <h1>IBN SINA (Avicenna)</h1>
Abu Ali al-Hussain Ibn Abdallah Ibn Sina(Avesina)
was born in 980 A.D. at Afshana near Bukhara,
the part of Iran. The young Bu Ali received his
early education in Bukhara, and by the age of
ten had become well versed in the study of the
Qur'an and various sciences. He started studying
philosophy by reading various Greek, Muslim and
other books on this subject and learnt logic and
some other subjects from Abu Abdallah Natili, a
famous philosopher of the time. While still young,
he attained such a degree of expertise in medicine
that his fame spread far and wide. At the age of 17,
he was fortunate in curing Nooh Ibn Mansoor,
the King of Bukhhara, of an illness in which all
the well-known physicians had given up hope. On
his recovery, the King wished to reward him, but
the young physician only desired permission to
use his uniquely stocked library.
<A HREF="#top"  style="font-size: 20pt;">Go Back to Top</A>
</pre>
</body>
</HTML>
```

From the above code you can see the topic **IBN SINA** (Avicenna) is marked as "top". **<A Name="top"></A>**. Then on the bottom of the page we link the top to the <a href....>. You can change the "top" to any another name as long as **<A Name="anything">**

When the user clicks on the Go back to Top, it will go to the exact mark. You can use this procedure anywhere in the page.

Here on the bottom of the page, we use a linkage which we call the top by using **<A HREF="#top" >**. This means go to the "top", which is already marked.

> ■▶ **Note:** The document must be larger than a page in order to go back to the top.

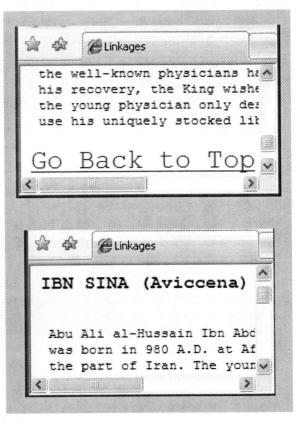

You may want to anchor to another page a file name such as *page2.html*, which is a completely different file: <A HREF=" Page2.html#topic2" > Go to Anchor </A>. The topic is marked as topic2 inside the page2.html.

Link to file

You may want to link your page to another page which is placed in the directory. In this case, try to create a text file and name it *Chapter2.html*
Copy and paste the text from the above example and make a link.

Example: 6.5
1.   <HTML><head>
2.   <title>Link to a file</title>
3.   </head><body>
4.   <A   href="Chapter2.html"   title="this goes to chapter 2">Chapter 2</A>.
5.   </body></HTML>

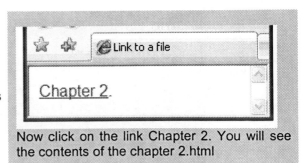

Now click on the link Chapter 2. You will see the contents of the chapter 2.html

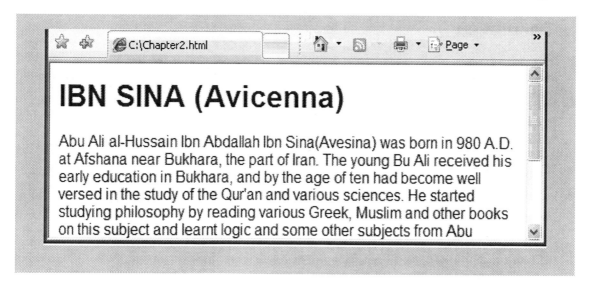

Tool Tip

The tool tip is a way to describe such items as the strings, buttons, labels and links. The tool tip is under the control of the mouse. Just put your mouse on the object and do not click. This will display the tool tip. We use the "title" in order to show the tool-tip.

<title="this is a tool tip">

You have already seen the tool-tip in the previous chapter which used "alt" instead of "title". You can use either "title" or "alt".

Example: 6.6

```
1.  <!DOCTYPE HTML PUBLIC "-//W3C//DTD HTML
    4.01//EN"
2.  "http://www.w3.org/TR/html4/Strict.dtd">
3.  <head>
4.  <title>Tool-Tip</title>
5.  <meta http-equiv="Content-Type" content
    ="text/html; charset=iso-8859-1">
6.  </head>
7.  <body>
8.  <p>
9.  <A href="chapter2.html" title="Click on Next Page
    to see chapter 2">Next page</A>.
10. <p>
11. </body>
12. </HTML>
```

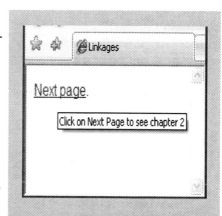

Just place your cursor on the "Next page button" and don't click to see the contents of the tool tip.

Decoration

HTML can get some help from CSS to decorate the text. So far any example related to the link produces a bar under the link. To remove the bar under the link you need to set text-decoration to "none", such as **style=text-decoration:none**. Look at this example which provides a link with a bar and a link without a bar.

Example: 6.7

```
1.    <!DOCTYPE HTML PUBLIC "-//W3C//DTD HTML 4.01//EN"
2.    "http://www.w3.org/TR/html4/Strict.dtd">
3.    <head>
4.    <title>Text-decoration</title>
5.    <meta http-equiv="Content-Type" content="text/html; charset=iso-8859-1">
6.    <style type="text/css"></style>
7.    </head>
8.    <body> <p>
9.    <a href="http://www.shanbedi.com">There is a bar under link</a>
10.   </p> <p>
11.   <a href="http://www.shanbedi.com" style="text-decoration:none" >There is no bar
      under link</a>
12.   </p> </body>
13.   </html>
```

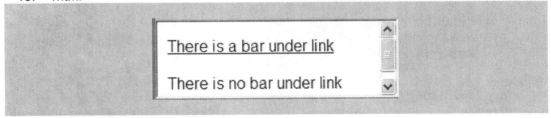

More CSS decoration

You can decorate the text further using underline, over line, line-through and blink (not supported by IE).

Example: 6.8

```
1.  <!DOCTYPE HTML PUBLIC "-//W3C//DTD HTML 4.01//EN"
2.  "http://www.w3.org/TR/html4/Strict.dtd">
3.  <head>
4.  <title>Text-decoration</title>
5.  <style type="text/css">
6.  h1 {text-decoration: overline}
7.  h2 {text-decoration: line-through}
8.  h3 {text-decoration: underline}
9.  </style>
10. <meta http-equiv="Content-Type" content="text/html; charset=iso-8859-1">
```

11.</head>
12.<body>
13.<h1> Line above text</h1>
14.<h2>Line through text</h2>
15.<h3> Underline text</h3>
16.</body> </HTML>

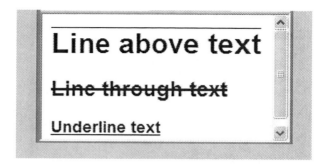

Link to images

Images can be used as a single image or a background image. You may want to load an image file as the background of your webpage or just load it as a family picture. You can also justify the size of an image to be displayed a little larger or smaller.

Example: 6.9
1. <!DOCTYPE HTML PUBLIC "-//W3C//DTD HTML 4.01//EN"
2. "http://www.w3.org/TR/html4/Strict.dtd">
3. <head>
4. <title>Image</title>
5. <meta http-equiv="Content-Type" content="text/html; charset=iso-8859-1">
6. </head>
7. <body> <p>
8. <A href="C:\\Eiffel.jpg"
9. title="Eiffel tower of Paris">Eiffel Tower</A>
10.</p></body> </HTML>

This picture has its original size, but you can control the width and the height of the image. In the next example, we will justify the size of the image.

Control images

The size of an image can be set to the desired size. You may adjust an image to a percentage number like 10%, or to just an integer number like 10. If you set an image to a percentage then it produces the image size relative to the page size.

Example: 6.10
1. <HTML> <head>
2. <title>Images size</title>
3. <body>   <h3>Voltaire   the   great   Philosopher(1778)</h3>
4. <img src="C:\\Voltaire.gif" align=right width=100   height=200   border=1 alt="Pic size 100X200">
5. <img   src="C:\\Voltaire.gif"   align=left width=30%   height=20%   border=1 alt="Pic size 30%X20%">
6.
<div   style="text-align: center;"><IMG SRC="C:\\Voltaire.gif" width=50 height=50 ALT="image in center"></div> </body> </HTML>

If we adjust the image size to 30%X20%, then we can see the small size. If we set the image size to 100X200, then the larger sized image is produced.

The **<div>** tag defines a division in a document. It automatically places a return or <br> on the document. It can be used like table layout or frame.

Adding text with images
You can adjust the image to be on the left or right and force the text to be wrapped around the image. The text can also be on the middle, top or bottom of the image.

Example: 6.11
1. <HTML> <head>
2. <title>Wrap text</title>
3. <body>   <b><center>Bertrand Russell(1872-1970),   Nobel   Prize   in 1950</center></b>
4. <img   src="C:\\russell.jpg"   align="left" width=40   height=50>   This   image   is adjusted to the left of the page. The text will be wrapped around the image.
5.

6. <img   src="C:\\russell.jpg"   align="right" width=40 height=50>This image is adjusted to the right of the page. The text will be

wrapped around the image. The image size is set to width = 40 and height = 50.
7. </body>
</HTML>

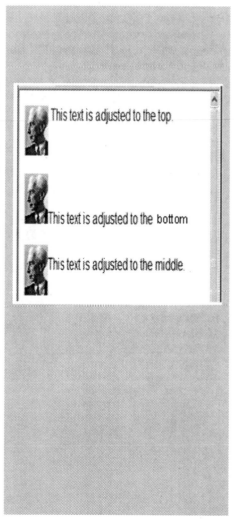

You can position the image related to the text around it in different modes like **middle**, **asbmiddle** (absolute middle), **top**, **texttop** (top text with top of the image), **bottom** and **baseline** (base of bottom line).

Example: 6.12

1. <HTML> <head>
2. <title>Wrap text</title>
3. <body>
4. <img   src="C:\\russell.jpg"   align="texttop" width=40 height=50> This text is adjusted to the top.
5.

6. <img   src="C:\\russell.jpg"   align="bottom" width=40 height=50>This text is adjusted to the bottom.
7.

8. <img   src="C:\\russell.jpg"   align="middle" width=40 height=50>This text is adjusted to the middle.
9.

10. <img src="C:\\russell.jpg" align= "absmiddle" width=40 height=50>This text is adjusted to the absmiddle.
11.

12. <img src="C:\\russell.jpg" align= "baseline" width=40 height=50>This text is adjusted to the baseline.
13. </body> </HTML>

You may want to use CSS code in your HTML code.
<div style="float: left;"><IMG SRC="pic.gif"> some texts</div>
<div style="float: right;"><IMG SRC="Pic.gif"> some texts</div>

You may use the **clear** attribute to clear one after the image.

<div style="float: right; clear: left;"><IMG src="pic.gif"></div>

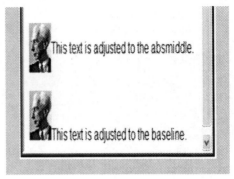

Spacing attributes

Images can be controlled by horizontal and vertical spacing. These spaces can be used to format an image with the surrounding text.

<img src="Pic.jpg" vspace="8" hspace="12">

Image as background

An image can be used as a webpage background. You may want to use a colored background. If so, use the color name <body bgcolor = "yellow">, color value (number) <body bgcolor="#FFCCFF"> or <body bgcolor="#582564">. To attach an image as a background, simply call the image's name on the <body background="pic.gif">.

Example: 6.13

1. <!DOCTYPE HTML PUBLIC "-//W3C//DTD HTML 4.01//EN"
2. "http://www.w3.org/TR/html4/Strict.dtd">
3. <head>
4. <title>Image Background</title>
5. <meta http-equiv="Content-Type" content="text/html; charset=iso-8859-1">
6. <style type="text/css">
7. body{ background-image: url('background1.gif');}

8. </style>
9. </head>
10. <body>
11. <p> </p>
12. </body>
13. </HTML>

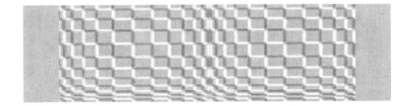

Review questions

1-What is an entity?

2-What entity produces tab space?

3- **<Body onLoad = "alert (' ')" >** is a correct statement.   True   False

4- How do you link to the top of the page?

5- How do you link an html file to the page?

6- h1 {text-decoration: none} What does this CSS produce?

7- Change the above code to create a bar over text.

8- Write a code to create horizontal and vertical spaces between text and an image.

9- Write a code to create a blue background.

10- Write a code to attach an image as the background.

Answers

1-An entity is used so that the browser doesn't get confused with HTML tags. For example, the signs of greater than "> "or less than ">" are similar to the HTML tags. Therefore, we must use "&glt" instead of ">".

2-

3-True

4- first use <name="x"> then **<A HREF="#X" >**

5- <A HREF="C:\\filename.html" >

6- Removes bar under the link text.

7- {text-decoration: overline}

8- <img src="Pic.jpg" vspace="8" hspace="12">

9- <body bgcolor="blue">

10-<body background="imge.jpg">

Chapter 7

Introduction

Layout plays an important role in webpage design. Usually, some layouts are done by using the pure table while others use frame. Both table and frame are great for creating webpage layouts, however both have some weaknesses. CSS is added to HTML in order to make codes shorter and to remove some problems related to styling table and frame. Frame divides the page into several portions and gives a better view with left or right navigation. In this chapter we will work on frame and the concept of HTML layout.

HTML Frame

Frame is a method of layout design in HTML. It allows multiple web pages to be open at the same time. Frame may provide a nice looking layout but it can be less useable with the presence of PHP. You use the **<frameset>** tag in order to provoke the fame. The frameset tag can be defined as rows and columns.

Horizontal frame

The horizontal frame means that all web pages line up horizontally. You can define the *frameset* to be displayed as several rows on the screen.

► **Note:** There are 3 files in the following example.
   Chap07.html which is a main file that has to be called (opened under browser).
   Frame1.html the top frame
   Frame2.html the bottom frame

► **Note:** The *DOCTYPE* is set to **Frameset.dtd**.

Save this file as **Main.html** then call it.

Example: 7.1
1. <!DOCTYPE HTML PUBLIC "-//W3C//DTD HTML 4.01//EN"
2. "http://www.w3.org/TR/html4/**Frameset**.dtd">
3. <head>
4. <title>Horizontal Frame</title>
5. <meta http-equiv="Content-Type" content="text/html; charset=iso-8859-1">
6. </head>
7. <frameset rows="50%,50%">
8. <frame src="frame1.html">
9. <frame src="frame2.html">
10. </frameset>
11. </html>

On the same directory, save the below file as **frame1.html**

1. <html>
2. <head>
3. <title>Frame1</title>
4. </head>
5. <body bgcolor="yellow">
6. This is Frame #1
7. </body>
8. </html>

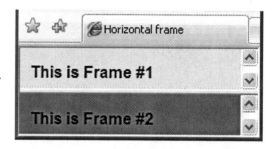

On the same directory, save this file as **frame2.html**

1. <html>
2. <head>
3. <title>Frame2</title>
4. </head>
5. <body bgcolor="Magenta">
6. This is Frame #2
7. </body>
8. </html>

The frameset tag is a command to perform a frame and the frame is a subset of the frameset which calls the two files (rame1.html and frame2.html).
<frame src="frame1.html">
<frame src="frame2.html">

Notice: You should have notice that the frameset contain no <body> section, the reason is that there are no text, link, object t be affected by it.

Vertical frame
The vertical frame is the same as the horizontal frame. We just change the *rows* to *cols* in order to provide two columns instead of two rows.

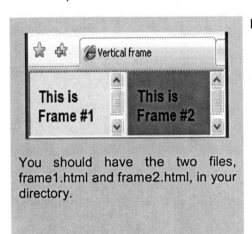

You should have the two files, frame1.html and frame2.html, in your directory.

Example: 7.2
1. <!DOCTYPE HTML PUBLIC "-//W3C//DTD HTML 4.01//EN"
2. "http://www.w3.org/TR/html4/**Frameset**.dtd">
3. <head>
4. <title>Vertical frame</title>
5. <meta http-equiv="Content-Type" content="text/html; charset=iso-8859-1">
6. </head>
7. <frameset cols="50%,50%">
8. <frame src="frame1.html">
9. <frame src="frame2.html">
10. </frameset>
11. </html>

Horizontal and Vertical Frames
You may want to combine both *columns* and *rows*. Here you can see two *cols* and two *rows,* but not in the matrix format. The two columns are placed on the top and a row is placed on the bottom.

Example: 7.3
Save as Frame.html
1. <!DOCTYPE HTML PUBLIC "-//W3C//DTD HTML 4.01//EN"
2. "http://www.w3.org/TR/html4/**Frameset**.dtd">
3. <head> <title>Multiple frames</title>
4. <meta http-equiv="Content-Type" content="text/html; charset=iso-8859-1">
5. </head> <frameset rows="25%,75%">
6. <frameset cols="50%,50%"> <frame src="frame1.html">
7. <frame src="frame2.html"> </frameset>
8. <frame src="frame3.html"> </frameset>
9. </html>

Save as Frame1.html
1. <html>
2. <head>
3. <title>Frame1</title>
4. </head>
5. <body bgcolor="yellow">
6. <b>This is Frame #1</b>
7. </body>
8. </html>

Save as Frame2.html
1. <html>
2. <head>
3. <title>Frame2</title>
4. </head>
5. <body bgcolor="Magenta">
6. <b>This is Frame #2</b>
7. </body>
8. <html>

Save as Frame3.html
1. <html>
2. <head>
3. <title>Frame3</title>
4. </head>
5. <body bgcolor="beige">
6. <b><center>This is Frame #3</b>
7. </body>
8. </html>

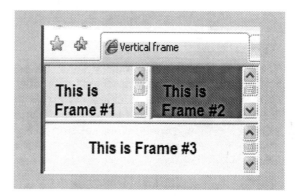

Most web pages usually use a format of two or three columns. The screen will be divided into two columns. One is small (navigating windows) and the other is big (Main windows). It could be 25% and 75%. All clickable items will be placed in the left frame.

Example: 7.4
1. <html> <head>
2. <title>Vertical frame</title>
3. </head>
4. <frameset cols="25%,75%">
5. <frame src="frame1.html">
6. <frame src="frame2.html">
7. </frameset>
8. </html>

Frame1.html and **frame2.html** must be in the directory.

The above example is adjusted to the left frame. It can also be on the right.

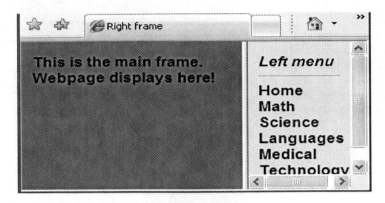

Scrollbar

The HTML frame automatically adds the scrollbar horizontally and vertically. When the contents of the page are bigger than the page size, the scrollbar becomes active. Otherwise, it is not visible. You can disable the scrollbar using **SCROLLBAR="NO"**.
You can use these attributes with your frame in HTML:

`<frame src="filename.html" noresize scrolling="no">`
`<frame src="Filename.html" scrolling="auto" noresize>`
`<frame src="Filename" scrolling="yes" noresize>`

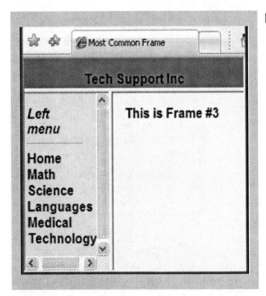

Example: 7.5

```
1.  <HTML>
2.  <HEAD>
3.  <TITLE>Most Common Frame</TITLE>
4.  </HEAD>
5.  <FRAMESET ROWS="15%, * ">
6.  <FRAME          SRC="frame1.html"
     SCROLLING=NO>
7.  <FRAMESET COLS="20%,80%">
8.  <FRAME SRC="frame2.html" >
9.  <FRAME SRC="frame3.html">
10. </FRAMESET>
11. </FRAMESET>
12. </HTML>
```

On line 5, you will see that the rows="15%, * " The star or asterisk sign allows you to generate an undefined size in the second row. This means the rest of page or, in this case, the total page minus 15%. You will see the "SCROLLING=NO" on line 6. This causes the scrollbar to be disabled, since the headline should not have a scrollbar.

Frame border

Frame can have a border. You may set the **border** width as border=#. The border can only be used by Netscape. The **Frameborder** = # is used to identify the border of a frame. Framesapacing =# sets up the space between frames.

Example: 7.6

<FRAMESET border="0" frameborder="0" **framespacing="10"** ROWS="15%,*">	<FRAMESET border="0" **frameborder="15"** framespacing="0" ROWS="15%,*">
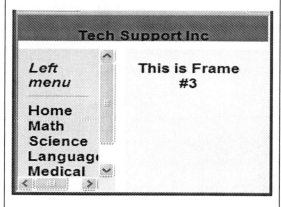	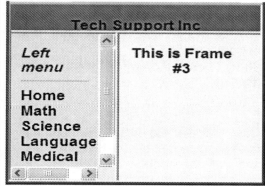
Look at the spacing which is set to **framespacing="10"** The border works under the Netscape browser.	Look at the border of the frame which is set to **frameborder="15"**

Target

This is a way to decide where the new windows must be placed. You can use these attributes to direct the opening file:

TARGET="_blank"
      Open in the blank window.
TARGET="_parent"
Open in the frame set that belongs to.
TARGET="_self"
      Open on the navigating frame.
TARGET="_top"
Takeover everything, it replace with all frame.

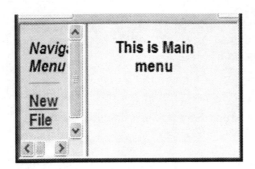

Example: 7.7
Save this as NewFile.html
1. <html>
2. <head>
3. <title>New frame</title>
4. </head>
5. <body bgcolor="Magenta">
6. <h2> The New File</h2>
7. <h3>   Placing   in   the   new windows</H3>
8. </body>
9. </html>

This is a code from **frame2.html,** the navigating frame.
<hr><a href=C:\\ newFrame.html> New File</a>

Now click on the New File from the navigating frame on the left. You will see that the content will open in the navigating window and NOT in the main windows. This is simply because the target is set to **_self** by default.

Load file into main menu
Most web users want to see that the new contents loading into the main windows and navigating parts remain untouched.
Steps:
1-On the main file (chap07.html) set the name of main frame (frame3.html) to content:
<FRAME name="**content**" SRC="frame3.html">
2-On the navigating frame (frame2.html) use base target="content" like:
<hr><a **base target="content"** href=NewFrame.html>New File</a>

Now look at all files.

Save as chap07.html 1. \<HTML\> 2. \<HEAD\> 3. \<TITLE\>Frame attributes\</TITLE\> 4. \</HEAD\> 5. \<FRAMESET COLS="20%,80%"\> 6. \<FRAME SRC="frame2.html" \> 7. \<FRAME name="content" SRC="frame3.html"\> 8. \</FRAMESET\> 9. \</HTML\>	**Save as frame2.html** this is the navigating frame. 1. \<html\> 2. \<head\> 3. \<title\>Frame2\</title\> 4. \</head\> 5. \<body bgcolor="yellow"\> 6. \<b\>\<I\>Navigation Menu\</I\> 7. \<hr\>\<a base target="content" href=NewFrame.html\>New File\</a\> 8. \</b\> 9. \</body\> 10. \</html\>
Save as **frame3.html** this main frame which NewFile must be open here! 1. \<html\> 2. \<head\> 3. \<title\>Frame3\</title\> 4. \</head\> 5. \<body bgcolor="beige"\> 6. \<b\>\<center\>This is Main menu\</b\> 7. \</body\> 8. \</html\>	**Save as NewFile.html** 1. \<html\> 2. \<head\> 3. \<title\>New frame\</title\> 4. \</head\> 5. \<body bgcolor="Magenta"\> 6. \<h2\> The New File\</h2\> 7. \<h3\> Place in new windows\</H3\> 8. \</body\> 9. \</html\>

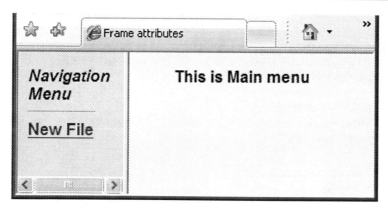

When you click on **NewFile** in the navigating window on the left, you will see that the new file will open in the main window without changing any navigation parts.

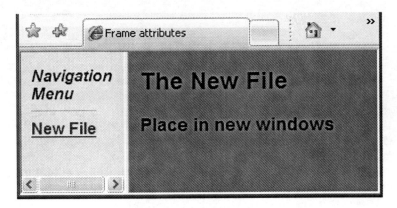

Layout

HTML itself does not provide a good layout. However, it provides a table layout which is used in many professional layouts.

We will try to create a layout similar to the above example which contains a banner part, a navigating part and a main part.

Should we use frames? Frame is little controversial, it is very nice and produces an easy look and feel, but it has several disadvantages. Search engine problem, browser support and some people may don't like it so they turn down their browser, these can be classified as disadvantages of using frames. We can create a complex frame without using **frame** or **table**; this can be done by power of **CSS** which you will see it on the example below.

Example: 7.8

```
1.  <!DOCTYPE HTML PUBLIC "-//W3C//DTD HTML 4.01//EN"
2.  "http://www.w3.org/TR/html4/Strict.dtd">
3.  <head>
4.  <title>CSS Frame</title>
5.  <meta http-equiv="Content-Type" content="text/html; charset=iso-8859-1">
6.  <style type= "text/css" >
7.  <!--
8.  #header {
9.  position: fixed;
10. width: 100%;
11. height: 50px;
12. top: 0;
13. left: 0;
14. background-color: #dbdb70;
15. color:maroon;
16. font-size:20px;
17. text-align:center;
18. font-weight:bolder;
19. }
```

```
20. #footer {
21. position: fixed;
22. bottom: 0;
23. left:0;
24. width: 100%;
25. height: 20px;
26. background-color: #dbdb70;
27. font-size:20px;
28. text-align:center;
29. font-weight:bold;
30. }
31. #navigator {
32. position: fixed;
33. top: 65px;
34. bottom: 20px;
35. left: 0px;
36. width: 160px;
37. background-color: #deb887;
38. bottom: 25px;
39. overflow: auto;
40. }
41. #webpage {
42. position: fixed;
43. left: 160px;
44. right: 0px;
45. top: 65px;
46. bottom: 25px;
47. background-color: #ffccff;
48. }
49. -->
50. </style>
51. </head>
52. <body>
53. <div id="header">This is Header of the frame</div>
54. <div id="navigator"><br> Java<br> PHP<br>MySQL<br>Ajax<br>This is
     navigator </div>
55. <div id="menu2">Second Menu </div>
56. <div id="webpage">Main webpage.</div>
57. <div id="footer">Footer of the frame</div>
58. </body>
59. </html>
```

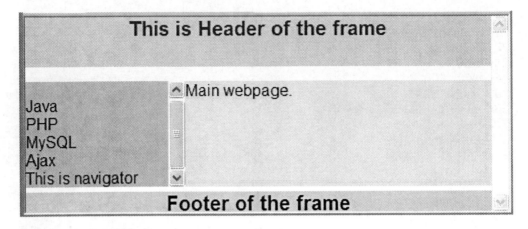

Notice that the scrollbar will active automatically.

    You see #navigator {
    position: fixed;
    top: 65px;
    bottom: 20px;
    left: 0px;
    width: 160px;}

The navigator is start from left(0) and its width is 160px so we must set the #webpage left to 160px which is a continuation of the navigator.

Review questions
1- Frame may not be a good option to use?   True   False
2- What is the horizontal frame?
3- How do you disable resize frame?
4- Can you set the frame navigator to the right side?   Yes   No
5- How do you disable the scrollbar in frame?
6- What is target ="_blank"?
7- What is the target="_top"?
8- Set framespace to 10.
9- By default the target is equal to _self.   True   False
10- Create a table layout with one small navigation window to the left and a main window to the right.

Answers
1-true
2-Contains only rows
3-<frame src="filename.html" **noresize**>
4- Yes
5- <frame src="filename.html" scrolling="no">
6- Opens a new window
7-Takeover all frames
8- <FRAMESET **framespacing="10"**>
9- True
10- See the last example

Chapter 8

Forms

Introduction

If are using any Internet programming language or scripts, you still need the HTML form. Rarely will you see a website that does not use the HTML form, especially when the site is dealing with online business. Form allows users to enter the complete information that is required by a company or individual sites. In fact, form is a combination of several HTML controls such as text field, text Area, checkbox, radio and password combo-box. In this chapter we will try to address all of the features which concern and are related to the form.

The form is widely used in website design. It provides input boxes that allow users to enter data into a webpage. For example, a text field allows a user to enter his name, ID or address. A password field can handle passwords in the form of asterisks (bullets) which is not a readable form of human language. The HTML form provides many different input options listed in the following chart.

HTML Form	
Textfield	Small textboxs to enter name, address, etc.
Password	Handle password(not readable)
Hidden	Hidden textfield(not displayed on screen)
Textarea	Cols and rows, to enter bigger texts
Checkbox	Option to check one or more item
Radio	Radio button, allows only one radio to check
Select option	Drop down menu, combo box
Submit button	Creates clickable button
Reset button	To reset field
Image button	To get image

The input tag is the simplest *form* format understood by the browser.
 <input> provides a box.
Example:
<form>
<input>
<input>
</form>

You see that the **<input>** tag creates two text fields (textboxes). Unless you control the layout, all text fields line up in one line by default.
Look at this example which creates two text fields: one for name and the other for ID.

Example: 8.1
1. <!DOCTYPE HTML PUBLIC "-//W3C//DTD HTML 4.01//EN"
2. "http://www.w3.org/TR/html4/Strict.dtd">
3. <head>
4. <title> Text Fields </title>
5. <meta http-equiv="Content-Type" content="text/html; charset=iso-8859-1">
6. </head>
7. <body>
8. <form action="" method="POST">
9. <p> Enter name:
10. <input type="text"   name="name">
11. </p>
12. <P> Enter ID:
13. <input type="text" name="ID">
14. </p> </form> </body>
15. </html>

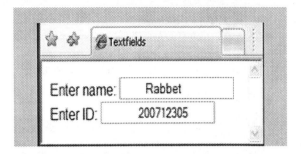

The ID box is not exactly lined up under the name in the text-field. This is because the length of "Enter name" is longer than the length of "Enter ID". Therefore, the text field is pushed to the right. The <input type="text"> tag creates a textbox.

Format text-field

In order to create a nice layout you need to use table. By using table you can adjust all textboxes on a line.

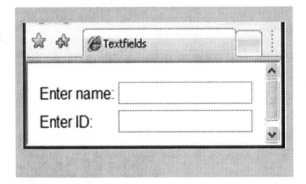

```
<html<body>
<form action="" method="POST">
<table border="0">
<tr><td>Enter name:</td>
<td><input type="text"
name="name"></td></tr>
<tr><td>Enter ID:</td>
<td><input type="text"
name="ID"></td></td>
</form> </table> </body> </html>
```

Text field size

Text field can have several attributes. For example, size=25 is the number of characters, and maxlength=10 means that the maximum length will be 10. Name, align, and tabindex also have attributes.

Size	Characters
maxlength	Maximum length
name	Name of field
value	Initial field value
align	alignment

Example: 8.2
1. <!DOCTYPE HTML PUBLIC "-//W3C//DTD HTML 4.01//EN"
2. "http://www.w3.org/TR/html4/Strict.dtd">
3. <head>
4. <title> limit Text Fields </title>
5. <meta http-equiv="Content-Type" content="text/html; charset=iso-8859-1">
6. </head>
7. <body>
8. <form action="" method="POST">
9. <table border="0">
10. <tr><td>Enter name:</td>
11. <td><input type="text" name="name" maxlength="10" size=20></td>
12. </tr> <tr>
13. <td>Enter Age:</td>
14. <td><input type="text" name="ID" size=2></td>
15. </table> </form> </body>
16. </html>

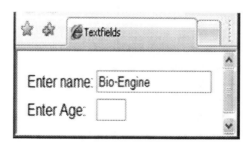

The maximum length of the first textbox is set to 10. When you try to enter the Bio-Engineering string, not all of the characters will show because it does not allow more than 10 characters in length. The textbox for *age* is set to *size=2*, so it is the size of only 2 characters.

Password

The password field is like text field except that it does not show the entry in a regular, readable way. Instead, it displays asterisks (*) or bullet shapes for each character that the user enters. You just need to write **type="password"** instead of **type="text"**.

Example: 8.3
```
1.  <!DOCTYPE HTML PUBLIC "-//W3C//DTD HTML 4.01//EN"
2.  "http://www.w3.org/TR/html4/Strict.dtd">
3.  <head>
4.  <title> Password Fields </title>
5.  <meta http-equiv="Content-Type" content="text/html; charset=iso-8859-1">
6.  </head>
7.  <body>
8.  <form action="" method="POST">
9.  <table border="0">
10. <tr><td>Enter password(4 to 7 chars)</td>
11. <td><input type="password" name="name" maxlength=7 size=10> </td></tr>
12. <tr><td>Enter password(4 to 9 chars)</td>
13. <td> <input type="password" name="pass" maxlength=9 value="" size="12" > </td>
14. </table> </form></body>
15. </html>
```

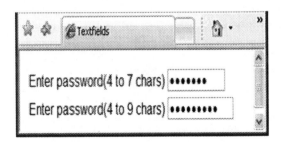

Hidden field

You can set the input tag to the **hidden** attribute: <input text=hidden>. This creates a box which never displays on the screen. What is the significance of the hidden box? The reality is that you need the hidden box for your database system. When you buy something on the Internet you fill in a form requiring such fields as your name, address, credit card, telephone and email, but you never enter the **date** and **time**. It must be an automatic field. The textbox exists but you do not see it. Look at this example in which a Visa card with be automatically entered into a database (but here we still do not have database).

Example: 8.4
```
1. <!DOCTYPE HTML PUBLIC "-//W3C//DTD HTML 4.01//EN"
2. "http://www.w3.org/TR/html4/Strict.dtd">
3. <head>
4. <title> Hidden Fields </title>
5. <meta http-equiv="Content-Type" content="text/html; charset=iso-8859-1">
6. </head>
7. <body>
8. <form action="" method="POST">
9. <table border="0">
```

10.   <tr><td>Enter name:</td>
11.   <td> <input type="text" name="name" maxlength=12 size=20 value="Hapoo Bampoo"></td></tr>
12.   <tr><td>
13.   <td> <input type="**hidden**" name="pass" maxlength=9 value=""size="12"> </td>
14.   </table> </form> </body>
15.   </html>

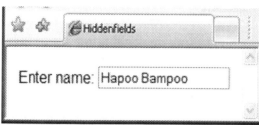

Anther text field exists but you do not see it. The hidden attribute does not allow you to see the textbox.

Text area

So far we have worked with Text-field (text), password field and hidden field. Now we will work on the **textarea**. Text area is similar to text field. The difference is that the text area can have rows and columns. The text area is usually bigger than the text field and used mostly for comments. The simple form of text area declaration: <TEXTAREA RWOS="5" COLS=20></TEXTAREA>

Example: 8.5
1. <!DOCTYPE HTML PUBLIC "-//W3C//DTD HTML 4.01//EN"
2. "http://www.w3.org/TR/html4/Strict.dtd">
3. <head>
4. <meta http-equiv="Content-Type" content="text/html; charset=iso-8859-1">
5. <title> Text Area </title>
6. </head>
7. <body>
8. <form action="" method="POST">
9. <table border="0"> <tr> <td> Enter name:</td>
10.   <td> <input type="text" name="name" size=20 value="This is TEXTFIELD"> </td> </tr>
11.   <tr><td>Enter your comments</td>
12.   <td> <textarea rows="5" cols="30" name="area">
13.   This is TEXTAREA
14.   </textarea>
15.   </td> </tr>
16.   </table> </form> </body>
17.   </html>

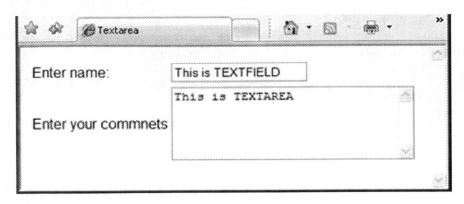

When you type text inside the text-area, it is automatically wrapped. This means that when your text reaches the end line it automatically returns back. However, you can set **wrap="off"** to not let text return. Wrap can be set to:

Off → wrapping off

Soft→ when you submit that there will not be any line break

Hard→ when you submit that there will not be any line break

Virtual→ by default the text wrap is set to virtual means, automatically wrapping. However when you send it, all text will be on one ongoing line.

Readonly

Sometimes you don't want to let the user change the contents of the text area. In this case you can use the **readonly = "readonly"**.

Example: 8.6
1. <!DOCTYPE HTML PUBLIC "-//W3C//DTD HTML 4.01//EN"
2. "http://www.w3.org/TR/html4/Strict.dtd">
3. <head>
4. <meta http-equiv="Content-Type" content="text/html; charset=iso-8859-1">
5. <title> Readonly attribute</title>
6. </head>
7. <body>
8. <form action="" method="POST">
9. <table border="0">
10.   <tr><td>Enter your comments</td>
11.   <td><textarea readonly="**readonly**" rows="5" cols="30" name="area">
12.   This is TEXTAREA however you can't change the contents
13.   </textarea>
14.   </td></tr>
15.   </table> </form></body>
16.   </html>

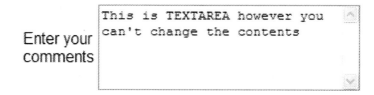

Enter your comments

You see the above text in the teat area is not changeable (user can't modify the text).

Checkbox

You can use a checkbox when you want to create multiple options which users can select. Checkboxes are little empty squares that are checkable with a mouse.
The **checked** value causes a checkbox to be automatically checked.

Example 8.7
1. <!DOCTYPE HTML PUBLIC "-//W3C//DTD HTML 4.01//EN"
2. "http://www.w3.org/TR/html4/Strict.dtd">
3. <head>
4. <meta http-equiv="Content-Type" content="text/html; charset=iso-8859-1">
5. <title> Checkbox</title>
6. </head>
7. <body>
8. <form action="" method="POST">
9. <p><b>Choose your courses</b>
10. </p>
11. <p><input type="checkbox" name="check1" value="Math"> Math
12. <input type="checkbox" name="check2" value="C#" > C# Coffee
13. <input type="checkbox" name="check3" value="Java" checked> Java
14. <input type="checkbox" name="check4" value="PHP" disabled> PHP
15. </p> </form> </body>
16. </html>

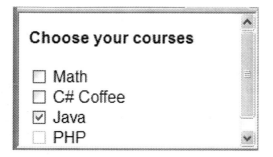

The large coffee is automatically checked. We set the *checked* attribute on line the related line. You will want the indicator to be on the right side of the checkbox, therefore you can modify the line as below:

Small Coffee <input type="checkbox" name="check1" value="Small" align="center">
. You see the PHP is not cheeked and it is **disabled**.

Radio button

The radio button allows for only one checkable radio at a time. In the case of gender, it can be either male or female.

Example 8.8

1. <!DOCTYPE HTML PUBLIC "-//W3C//DTD HTML 4.01//EN"
2. "http://www.w3.org/TR/html4/Strict.dtd">
3. <head>
4. <meta http-equiv="Content-Type" content="text/html; charset=iso-8859-1">
5. <title> Radi button</title>
6. </head>
7. <body>
8. <form action="" method="POST">
9. <p> <b> Are you older than 65</b>
10. </p>
11. <p>
12. <input type="radio" name="radio1" value="yes" > YES
13. <input type="radio" name="radio2" value="no" > NO
14. <input type="radio" name="radio3" value="65"checked> 65 year
15. <input type="radio" name="radio4" value="105" disabled>100 and more...
16. </p></form> </body>
17. </html>

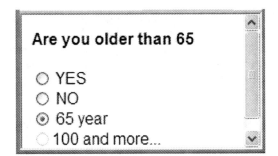

Dropdown menu

The drop-down menu is a combo box that allows you to list several options. The user can select one item at a time from the options. The combo box is small and you can place many items inside the combo box. When the user clicks on the combo box it drops down and all the items are visible. The drop down list is efficient simply because it doesn't occupy much space on the webpage. To create a combo box in HTML you use the **<select>** tag. For each item to be added you must use the <option> tag. See the following example.

Example: 8.9

```
1.  <!DOCTYPE HTML PUBLIC "-//W3C//DTD HTML 4.01//EN"
2.  "http://www.w3.org/TR/html4/Strict.dtd">
3.  <head>
4.  <meta http-equiv="Content-Type" content="text/html; charset=iso-8859-1">
5.  <title> Combo-box</title>
6.  </head>
7.  <body>
8.  <form action="" method="POST">
9.  <p>
10. <b> Select an item!</b>
11. </p>
12. <div>
13. <select name="items">
14. <option value= op1 > Milk </option>
15. <option value= op2> Onions </option>
16. <option value= op3 > Bananas </option>
17. <option value= op4> Grapes </option>
18. <option value= op5> Oranges </option>
19. </select>
20. </div> </form> </body>
21. </html>
```

You can select which item displays first when the page is loaded.
<option value= op3 *selected*> Banana</option>
In this instance when the page is loaded, bananas will be on the top.

If you want three items shown when the page is loaded then set size=3.

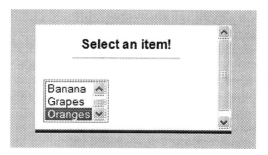

<select name="selecto" **size=3**>

If you disable the combo box then the user can't change anything.

<select name="selecto" size=5 **disabled**>

The *READONLY* option causes the combo box to be readable but not changeable.

<select name="selecto" size=3 **READONLY**>

Submit Button

The <input type="submit"> tag creates a submit button. When the user presses the button, all the contents of the form must be submitted to the address that is declared within that form. So far you created a simple form. However, a form must have a name, action and a post. Look at this form.

<form   name="SomeName"   action   =   "http://www.shanbedi.com/file.php" method="POST">

- Name is the name of the form which you must call later.
- Action means what type of action and where the form is to be submitted.
- Post means the type of sending, whether **POST** or **GET** (you will learn it in the PHP book).

Example: 8.10
1. <!DOCTYPE HTML PUBLIC "-//W3C//DTD HTML 4.01//EN"
2. "http://www.w3.org/TR/html4/Strict.dtd">
3. <head>
4. <meta http-equiv="Content-Type" content="text/html; charset=iso-8859-1">
5. <title> Submit button</title>
6. </head> <body>
7. <form action="" method="POST">
8. <div>
9. Enter name: <input type="text" size="20" value="Enter your name here!">
10. Enter email: <input type="text" size="20" value="Enter your Email here!">
11.
<input type="submit" value="Send ">
12. </div> </form> </body>
13. </html>

Enter name: Enter your name here!

Enter email: Enter your Email here!

Send

```
<input type="submit" value="Send ">
```
In fact, the value is the caption of the button.

OOPS: Why is there no response when I click on the button? The reality is that you are working on the client side, so the content of the form is not submitted anywhere.

Look at another example with a little message.

Example: 8.11

```
1.  <!DOCTYPE HTML PUBLIC "-//W3C//DTD HTML 4.01//EN"
2.  "http://www.w3.org/TR/html4/Strict.dtd">
3.  <head>
4.  <meta http-equiv="Content-Type" content="text/html; charset=iso-8859-1">
5.  <title> Submit button</title>
6.  </head> <body>
7.  <form action="" method="POST">
8.  <p> Enter name: <input type="text" size="20" value="Enter your name here!"> <br>
9.  Enter email: <input type="text" size="20" value="Enter your Email here!"> <br>
10. <br><input type="submit" value="Send " onClick="alert('Contents of form must be
    submitted \rto the server, but we are not\r connected to the  server!');" >
11. </p> </form> </body>
12. </html>
```

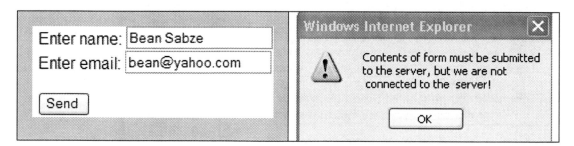

The form must be submitted to the server and then get some responses from the server. Here we try to send information and get an answer back. You see the message warning about connection which simply tells your website is not connected to server or databases.

This form adds two numbers even though it can't usually add numbers unless we specify the server name.

For the purpose of this exercise we create a **PHP** file on our server to fulfill your request. When you press the submit button, the contents of the form (num1 and num2) will be posted to the file which already exists on the server. Therefore, you receive your appropriate response.

Example: 8.12

1. <!DOCTYPE HTML PUBLIC "-//W3C//DTD HTML 4.01//EN"
2. "http://www.w3.org/TR/html4/Strict.dtd">
3. <head>
4. <meta http-equiv="Content-Type" content="text/html; charset=iso-8859-1">
5. <title> Adding Numbers</title>
6. </head> <body>
7. <form name= " add" action= "http://www.shanbedi.com/adding.php">
8. <p> Enter number 1
9. <input type=text name="num1">
10. Enter number 2
11. <input type=text name="num2">
12. <input type=submit value="Calculate Sum">
13. </p>
14. </form>
15. </body>
16. </html>

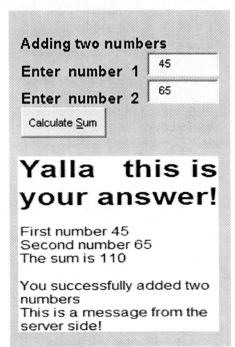

When you run the above file, you will see it nicely adding two numbers. The file **adding.php** exists inside the server and it is provoked by line 7.

Email

Usually we use "**mailto**" to perform email in HTML. However, mailto may not be a good option since it can be found by spammers. You may want to use some kind of encoding or direct form of mail. Here we will look at the *mailto* option.

▶ **Note:** Your email editor program must be set up prior to sending email. Outlook or any another such program must already be in your system.

Example: 8.13

1. <!DOCTYPE HTML PUBLIC "-//W3C//DTD HTML 4.01//EN"
2. "http://www.w3.org/TR/html4/Strict.dtd">
3. <head>
4. <meta http-equiv="Content-Type" content="text/html; charset=iso-8859-1">
5. <title> Email</title>
6. </head>
7. <body>
8. <form action="" method="POST">
9. <p><a href="mailto:office@macgill.edu"> Send Email</a></p>

10.</form>
11.</body>
12.</HTML>

mailto with subject
It displays subject

📧 To:	me@you.com
📧 Cc:	
Subject:	Dating time!

<a href="mailto:me@you.com?
subject =Dating time!"> Send Email </a>

mailto with copy

📧 To:	office@ubi.edu
📧 Cc:	Peter@ubi.EDU
Subject:	

<a href="mailto:office@ubi.edu?cc=
Peter@ubi.edu "> Send Email </a>

mailto with blind copy

📧 To:	office@utu
📧 Cc:	
📧 Bcc:	Sami@utu.com
Subject:	

<a href="mailto:office@utu?bcc=
Sami@utu.com ">Send Email</a>

Body Multi-lines message!

<a href="mailto:admin@uc.com?body=I am
going to invite you for a
%0A%0A Camel riding in my apartment
%0A%0A this afternoon at 3:50 !">Send
mail</a>

Remember: Use "%0A" for a new line, and use " %0A%0A" for double line.

Put them all together

<a href="mailto:office@uu.com?subject =
Join Staff &cc=peter@uu.com&
bcc=Jack@JackLondon.edu">Send mail</a>

You use only one ?(question mark) and combining several objects with amps "&"

Review questions

1. What is the simple tag to create a form?
2. Write a tag to create a password field.
3. Write a tag to create a text field.
4. Write a tag to create a text area.
5. Write a tag to create a combo box.
6. Show three items in a combo box (select)
7. What is the difference between the <select> tag and the <option> tag?
8. What is the difference between a checkbox and a radio box?
9. How do you create a submit button?
10. What happens if you press the submit button?

Answers

1. <form> </form>
2. <input type="password">
3. <input type="text">
4. <TEXTAREA rows="5" cols="30" name="area">
5. <Select> </select>
6. <select name="combo" **size=3**>
7. Select tag creates a combo box, whereas with the option tag you add elements to the combo box.
8. Checkbox allows you to check one or several options; radio allows you to check only one element.
9. <input type=submit value=" Sum">
10. The contents of the form must be posted to the server and from there receive the answer (responses).

Chapter 9

Multimedia

Introduction

What is multimedia? Multimedia refers to multiple communications: videos, sounds, texts, animated graphics and images delivered via communicating lines or electronic devises. Multimedia is all about communicating in many different ways. As technology progresses, multimedia has grown to be part of modern communication. Everyone wants to see some sort of multimedia, such as video clips or music, embedded in the website.

HTML has the capability to embed audio, video, simple images or animated graphics through the <embed> tag. However, the standard tag is **<object>**.

▶ **Note:** The <embed> tag has been deprecated (meaning it is no longer used) in favor of <object>. In fact, the <object> tag acts as multipurpose in HTML. Object refers to all the elements which have to be embedded in the HTML code.

Embedding text

Text can be embedded into HTML very easily. First you need to create a text file. For example, open your notepad and try to type some text which you will then save as Test.txt.

Now create your HTML file and embed your text file inside the HTML file.

Example: 9.1

Save as **Test.txt**
In notepad

This is the text that is embedded in an HTML file. We set size, attributes and type of the text in the HTML file.

Save as: **Embed.html** and run it.
1. <HTML><head><Title> Embedding Text</Title></head> <body>
2. <H2>Maim website with Text file!</H2>
3. <object data="c:\test.txt" type="text/plain" width="300" height= "200" >
4. </object> </body>
5. </HTML>

Maim website with Text file!

```
This is the text that is embedded
We set size , attributes and type
in the HTML file.
```

Embedding HTML file

You can embed an HTML file directly to your website. First create an HTML file and save it with an HTML extension. Save it as **Test.html** then call it into the main webpage.
Now open notepad and save this file as **Test.html**

```
<HTML>
<body bgcolor="yellow">
I am an HTML file and I am embedded into an HTML
website! They gave me a size to be: 300 X 200. If I am
attached to many other texts then the scrollbar
automatically becomes active!
<body>
</HTML>
```

Now create your main *HTML* file as below, save it as **embed.html** and run it.

```
<HTML><head><Title> Embedding</Title></head>
<body>
<H1>This is the main  website</H1>
<object data="test.html" type="text/html" width="300" height="200">
</object>
</body>
</HTML>
```

This is the main website

Embedding an image

An image can be loaded along with the HTML page. It can be done by using img and a source tag like <img src=file.jpg>. You can use some attributes to identify the size of the image.
<img src="PicFile.gif" width="150" height="60">

From a website or *different location*:
<img src="http://yahoo.com/folder/image.jpg">

You can add tool tip:
<img src="Cat.jpg" alt="This is Persian cat!">

Image formats

There are several image formats identified by extensions such as (**.gif**) or (**.jpg**). These four formatted images are used most often with today's Internet, with all browsers treating them well:

- **GIF**
- **JPEG or JPG**
- **PNG**
- **BMP**

Extension	Name	Description
.gif	Graphics Interchange Format	This graphics file format was used by *CompuServe* in the late 1980s. GIF supports 256 color monitors. This image is easily used in WWW.
.jpg or **.jpeg**	Joint **P**hotographic **E**xperts **G**roup	JPEG is used for color images and is especially used for photos and scanning. The jpg size is smaller compared to the gif. It is familiar for most browsers.
.png	Portable Network Graphics	This new graphics format is similar to the GIF. It is designed to replace the gif. Presently all browsers handle it well.
.bmp	BitMaPped graphic	This graphics format is used in the Windows. It can be created simply by MS-paint. We usually do not use .bmp on an image for the Internet. However, some parts like counter are in the bmp format.

Image map

Image map is one of the most interesting and amazing parts of HTML. Simply put, the image map is one image with multiple clickable areas. How is this possible? First you have to have a good image with distinct regions. You must also calculate the coordination for each region on the image (mapping). The target must be clearly identified.

Image Shapes

You can play with three different shapes:
Rect: rectangular shapes calculate top-right, bottom-left.
Circle: circular format; you need to calculate coordinate and radius (half of diameter).
Polygon: polygon shapes (many shapes); you need to calculate coordinates carefully.

Map name

In order to avoid confusion when using several maps, you need to name them properly. For example:

```
<IMG SRC="Toyota.gif" USEMAP="#Car1">
<IMG SRC="BMW.gif" USEMAP="#Car2">
```

```
<map name="Car1">
The related cod!
</map>
<map name="Car2">
The related code!
</map>
```

Map target

To complete mapping the regions, you need to use some HTML keywords: "**area**", "**shape**", "**usemap**" and "**coordes**", along with the related **link**.

Example: 9.2
1. <!DOCTYPE HTML PUBLIC "-//W3C//DTD HTML 4.01//EN"
2. "http://www.w3.org/TR/html4/Strict.dtd">
3. <head>
4. <meta http-equiv="Content-Type" content="text/html; charset=iso-8859-1">
5. <title> Mapping</title>
6. </head>
7. <body> <p>
8. <img src="mapping.jpg" usemap="#DC" ALT="One image with two areas">
9. <map name="DC">
10. <area shape="circle" coords="90,30,30" href="http://www.moon.com"
11. alt="Click on circle">
12. <area shape="rect" coords="169,60,18,139" href="http://www.land.com"
13. alt="Click on Rectangle">
14. </map> </p></body>
15. </HTML>

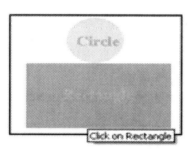

The above image is only one image divided into two parts: a *circle* and a rectangle shapes. By clicking on the circle, you will see a website and by clicking on the rectangle, you will see another website.

We use an attribute such as *usemap* in order to assign it to the name tag later. The above example works perfectly.
But **wait a minute**, how did you calculate the exact coordinates?

Well, you can open your image in any image editor and it will show the coordinates. Here, we made this simple image in Photoshop and it gave us the exact coordinates.

For a rectangle, you just need to type the number of the top-right and the number of the bottom-left (4 points).
For a circle, you need the two points **X, Y** and the **radius** of the clickable object.

Audio and Video

When we talk about multimedia, sound and video cross our minds. "Listening" and "Watching" are both important for humans. These can be done with the power of multimedia systems.

Adding sounds

First you have to have a sound file in your computer (download a file and save it on your disk). Then you must call this file through the HTML embedding format. There are almost three ways to add sound (audio) to your website or your page.
The three formatted tags, **<object>**, **<embed>** and **<bgsound>**, help you to add sounds. The sound file may have an extension, such as **.wav, .mid, .mp3** or **.au**, but these four extensions are the more popular and useable in today's multimedia programs. Let's first use the embed tag to add sound on our page.
<embed src="filename.wav" width=" xx " height="xx" autoplay="false" hidden="false" loop="false" volume="xx"></embed>**

If **autopaly** is set to true then it automatically starts.
If you set **hidden=true** then the box will not be shown.
If **loop** is set to true then it will be looped.
Volume can be from 1 to 100. By default it is set to 50.

In addition you can use the **direct link** like:
<A HREF="http://www.mydomain.com/sounds/soundfile.mid">Listen to song</A>

There has always been problem regarding embedding the sound into the website.
The <bgsound>tag is not a valid HTML or XHTML but works in IE
The <embed> tag is not a valid HTML or XHTML tag, but it works in most browsers.
The <object> - a valid HTML and XHTML tag, but it works in some browsers. It is the new XHTML object.

After you see the above image, try to click on the play icon to produce music.

Example: 9.3 Not validated but works
```
<HTML><head><Title> Embedding Sounds</Title></head>
<body>
<embed src="Banan.wav" width=" 140 " height="30"
autoplay="false" hidden="false" loop="false"
volume="60"></embed>
</body>
</HTML>
```

If you set the *autoplay* to true then it automatically produces a sound. Instead of autoplay you may set the **autostart** to **"false"**
You can play sound with the **Meta tag**. The Meta tag has to be inside the head tag.

Example: 9.4 not validated but works
```
<HTML><head> <Title> Meta Sounds</Title>
<meta http-equiv="REFRESH" content="0;URL='./Golpa.wav?autostart=true'">
</head> <body> </body>
</HTML>
```

Sounds from the website
You can listen to the sound that already exists on your server. Simply write a short program in pure HTML and run it. Look at this song to which you are listening directly from the website. We use the embed tag.

It should start automatically.

Example: 9.5 Not validated, works
1. `<HTML><head>`
2. `<Title> Embedding Sounds</Title>`
3. `</head>`
4. `<body>`
5. `<p>Listen to Music<br>`
6. `<embed            allowScriptAccess="never"            src= "http://www.shanbedi.com/Music/Homeira.mp3"`
7. `height="50" width="150" autostart="true" loop="false">`
8. `</embed> </body> </HTML>`

Using HTML <object>
Earlier we mentioned that <embed> has been deprecated in favor of the **<object>** tag, which provides more functions. Consequently, we should no longer be using <embed>.

What is wrong with <embed>?
As you can see, the format for embed is **<embed src =" "/>** and the format for object is **<object data= " " > ...</object>**.

Is there something wrong with the <embed> tag? The reality is that there are different browsers out there, each implementing HTML codes differently. The embed tag was first introduced by Netscape Navigator 2 and it has never become an HTML standard. One of the major problems is that when you leave a page and try to visit another page, it ends without user permission. This causes problems for those who may want to visit several websites or pages and listen to their favorite music.

List of some important browsers

Mozila FireFox	Mozilla is an open source project, including Firefox and Minimo Mobile Browser. It comes from the old Netscape.
Microsoft Internet Explorer (IE)	Comes from Microsoft.
Konqueror	Unix-based Web browser.
Safari	KHTML-based web for Apple Computers and is optimized for Mac OS X.
Opera	Browser support for **BitTorrent** with multiple search engines.

Add Music using object

The <embed> tag is used by **Mozilla**-based browsers, including different versions of Firefox browsers. The <object> tag is used by Internet Explorer-based browsers. Occasionally, you may be forced to use them both in order to serve different browsers. The <object> tag is known and supported by **W3C Consortium**. **Param** means parameter which can be used with several attributes.

```
<!DOCTYPE HTML PUBLIC "-//W3C//DTD HTML 4.01//EN"
"http://www.w3.org/TR/html4/Strict.dtd">
 <head>
 <meta http-equiv="Content-Type" content="text/html; charset=iso-8859-1">
<title> Embedding Sounds using Object</title>
 </head> <body> <p>
<object data="homeira.wav" type="audio/x-wav" title="Classic Music">
<param name="autostart" value="false"/>
<param name="hidden" value="true"/>
<a href="sound.html">Music</a>
</object> </p> </body>
</html>
```

The classic attribute is a number (32 bits) and is a unique identifier for the necessary **ActiveX** control. It tells which ActiveX should be downloaded. Flash Player uses **clsid:D27CDB6E-AE6D-11cf-96B8-444553540000**, for example.
The format is 8-4-4-4-12 digits.
In this example we use **clsid:6BF52A52-394A-11D3-B153-00C04F79FAA6**
for both movies and music.

Example: 9.6
1. <!DOCTYPE HTML PUBLIC "-//W3C//DTD HTML 4.01//EN"
2. "http://www.w3.org/TR/html4/Strict.dtd">
3. <head>
4. <meta http-equiv="Content-Type" content="text/html; charset=iso-8859-1">
5. <title> Object Sounds</title>
6. </head> <body>
7. <p>Music using object embedding
8. <object id = "Mediaplayer" height = "300" width = "300" classid = "clsid:6BF52A52-394A-11D3-B153-00C04F79FAA6" >
9. <param name = "URL" value = "Homeira.mp3" >
10. <param name = "autoStart" value = "true" >
11. <param name="Showstatusbar" value="true">
12. <param name="Autorewind" value="True">
13. </object> </body>
14. </HTML>

<param name = "uiMode" value = "full" > When the player is set to full, it shows all necessary values. It can be set to visible, mini, none, full and so on.

Listen to Music using object
You can listen to music from your website using object. Change line 6 on the above example to this path:
<param name = "URL" value = "http://www.shanbedi.com/Music/Homeira.mp3" >

Combination of <embed> and <object>
We know that there are many different browsers which can be used. Unfortunately, each browser acts differently. For example, of the two most important browsers, Mozilla Firefox

and IE, one uses embed while the other uses object, therefore we may need to use both within the same code.

We use both the <embed> and the <object> tags.
The <embed> tag is NOT a HTML or XHTML tag; so it will not pass *validator*. The <object> tag passes the *validator* and it is known for Validator.w3.org

Example: 9.7
1. <!DOCTYPE HTML PUBLIC "-//W3C//DTD HTML 4.01//EN"
2. "http://www.w3.org/TR/html4/Strict.dtd">
3. <head>
4. <meta http-equiv="Content-Type" content="text/html; charset=iso-8859-1">
5. <title> Both embed & Object</title>
6. <body> <p> Embed & Object
7. <object id = "MediaPlayer" height = "300" width = "300" classid = "clsid:6BF52A52-394A-11D3-B153-00C04F79FAA6" >
8. <param name = "URL" value = "http://www.shanbedi.com/Music/Homeira.mp3" >
9. <param name = "autoStart" value = "true" >
10. <param name="Showstatusbar" value="true">
11. <param name="Autorewind" value="True">
12. <embed allowScriptAccess="never" src= "http:// www.shanbedi.com/Music/Homeira.mp3"
13. height="50" width="150" autostart="true" loop="false">
14. </embed> </object> </body>
15. </HTML>

Watch movie

The simple way to see a movie is to use the old code which downloads the file completely. In this way, you automatically see the video.

Example: 9.8
1. <!DOCTYPE HTML PUBLIC "-//W3C//DTD HTML 4.01//EN"
2. "http://www.w3.org/TR/html4/Strict.dtd">
3. <head>
4. <meta http-equiv="Content-Type" content="text/html; charset=iso-8859-1">
5. <title> Movie</title>
6. </head>
7. <body>
8. <p> Simple Video Downloading
9. <a href=http://www.shanbedi.com/Music /Shebo.wmv >
10. See this video </a> </p>
11. </body> </HTML>

Simple video

You may see the video WMV extension the same way as you would with music. Here we try to attach a video file to our HTML code. You will see the video by running this program.

Example 9.9

```
1. <!DOCTYPE HTML PUBLIC "-//W3C//DTD HTML 4.01//EN"
2. "http://www.w3.org/TR/html4/Strict.dtd">
3. <head>
4. <meta http-equiv="Content-Type" content="text/html; charset=iso-8859-1">
5. <title> Movie</title>
6. </head>
7. <body>
8. <p> Watching Video <br>
9. <object id = "MediaPlayer" height = "300" width = "300" classid = "clsid:6BF52A52-
   394A-11D3-B153-00C04F79FAA6" >
10. <param name = "URL" value = "Hassan.wmv" >
11. <param name = "autoStart" value = "true" >
12. <param name="Showstatusbar" value="true">
13. <param name="Autorewind" value="True">
14. <embed allowScriptAccess="never" src= "Shebo.wmv"
15. height="300" width="300" autostart="true" loop="false">
16. </embed> </object> </body>
17. </HTML>
```

To position your video on the right use align="right". You can use the <div> tag to bring the video to the center.

<div align = "center" >
<object id = "MediaPlayer" height = "150" width = "100"
classid = "clsid:6BF52A52-394A-11D3-B153-00C04F79FAA6">
<param name = "URL" value = "Shebo.wmv" ></div>. Use CSS codes to position to the exact desired point.

Adding an applet animation

It is simple to add an applet (java) *animation* or image to the website. You must add the compiled object of applet, which is a "class" extension. You simply write a code such as

*<Applet Code="**AppletFile.class**" width=300 Height=300>*
</Applet>

Laboratory exercises

1- Download an image of a Canadian map and then map at least 4 provinces. When you click on BC, it will display the BC provincial map or if you click on Ontario, it will display the map of Ontario.

2- Write a code that embeds a video. For the purpose of IE, use the <object> tag. You may want to have access to the video by using the website.

3- Download an applet animation from a free site and then attach it to the website.

Next:
HTML was so easy I learned it completely. So now what do I have to do? Now that you have completed the HTML *client side* you need to learn a *little more* to advance your *client side* coding. We have added the CSS which you certainly need in order to master your knowledge.

Part II
CSS

Chapter 10

Introduction to CSS

Introduction

In previous chapters we mentioned that some parts of HTML are deprecated, meaning that they are not supported and we should not use them. In this regard, CSS (Cascading Style Sheet) replaces the deprecated features. CSS is a modern way of creating a webpage. It is easy and faster to use. The source code becomes smaller than the regular pure HTML codes. You can design styles once and use it many times. In some previous chapters you learned some parts of CSS, especially colors and fonts. We will look at CSS more thoroughly in this chapter. You must have full knowledge of HTML prior to this point.

Formatting Text

Text can be formatted with such features as fonts, colors, and text background. Font and color are easy to implement in CSS, whether inline or by pre-style set in the head.

Cascading Style Sheets

Cascading Style Sheet or just Style Sheet (widely known as CSS) helps you to master your client webpage. It removes some of the weakness of HTML. An advantage of the CSS is that the code becomes significantly shorter. You can create your style inside the head tag and use it for an entire page or pages. You do not need to declare style again and again and, therefore, the code becomes significantly short. To start CSS you need to know the style itself. Style-sheet can be an internal or external style. The internal style can be body style (entire style) or **Inline** style.

Cascading Style Sheet CSS		
Internal Style	**Body Style**	**Inline style**
	Style for the entire body of the page with the same properties as color, font, background, etc.	Style that is used for individual lines inside the code.
External style	Enables us to call an external file of CSS, *filename.css*	

Selector

The selector is the base of CSS. The selector allows you to use your style. The basic selector uses HTML tags like *H1, H2, P, and B*. The general format of selector is:

General Format	Selector	Property	Value
Example	P	{ color :	blue ; }

For example:
H1 {color: yellow ;}
In one of the previous chapters you saw and worked with *CSS* color and font. Here we will use them quickly and then move to the next section.
The style must be placed inside the head:

```
<Head>
<style type="text/css">
 body { color: blue;  }
</style>
</Head>
```

You can use **multiple properties** like color and background. There can be two or more properties in the same selector such as fonts, colors, background, borders, text formatting and link.

```
<Head>
<style type="text/css">
 body { color: blue; background: yellow; }
</style>
</Head>
```

The selector (body) contains two properties: color and background.
This example makes the entire body background yellow with some blue text.

Example: 10.1
1. <!DOCTYPE HTML PUBLIC "-//W3C//DTD HTML 4.01//EN"
2. "http://www.w3.org/TR/html4/Strict.dtd">
3. <head>
4. <meta http-equiv="Content-Type" content= "text/html; charset=iso-8859-1">
5. <title> Color and background</title>
6. <style type="text/css">
7. body { color: blue; background: yellow; }
8. </style> </head>
9. <body> <p>
10. Everything you type here will be in blue!
11. With yellow background!
12. </p> </body>
13. </html>

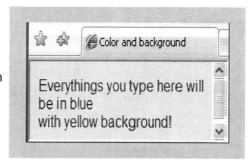

In the above example, we declared **body {color: blue; background: yellow; }** inside the head. The selector name is **body**. Therefore, the entire body of the page will accept the style.

Grouping selector
Selector can be grouped in several tags. For example, you can use it if you want to use different size or bold and so on.
H1, H2, h5, b, I {font-family: Tahoma, Verdana, Arial ;}

Inline style
When you create a style and place it within the head, the entire body of code obeys the pre-set style. What happens if you want to create some new style later? You must change the line of code with a different style (use **inline** style).
<p style="color: #CCCCCC;">The new formatted text</p>

Example: 10.2
1. <!DOCTYPE HTML PUBLIC "-//W3C//DTD HTML 4.01//EN"
2. "http://www.w3.org/TR/html4/Strict.dtd">
3. <head> <meta http-equiv="Content-Type" content="text/html; charset=iso-8859-1">
4. <title> Inline Style</title>

5. <style type="text/css">
6. b{ font-size: 14pt; color: red; }
7. </style> </head> <body> <p>
8. <b>This is a pre-style text in red</b> </p>
9. <H4 style="color: #CCCCCC;"> The inline
    style text in CCCCCC</H4>
10. </body>
11. </html>

You will see that the **inline** style generates different colors. You can use **class** and **ID** in order to do the same thing, which we will learn later.

Now you are familiar with the HTML selector. The HTML selector means using the HTML tags name as a *selector* name. As already mentioned, there is also the **CLASS** selector and the **ID** selector.
With either external or internal styles, the selector can be classified as:

Selectors:	*HTML selector(P,I,B and so on)* *Class selector* *ID selector*

Class selector
Previously we used the HTML selector with a preset style or inline style. Now we will use the CLASS selector. The class selector is good since you don't have to redefine the HTML selector entirely. In fact, you just use different styles within the source code. The general syntax for the CLASS selector:
.ClassSelector{property : value; }

> ▶ **Note:** There is a *dot* in front of the selector.

Example: 10.3
1. <!DOCTYPE HTML PUBLIC "-//W3C//DTD HTML 4.01//EN"
2. "http://www.w3.org/TR/html4/Strict.dtd">
3. <head>
4. <meta http-equiv="Content-Type" content="text/html; charset=iso-8859-1">
5. <title> Class Selector</title>
6. <style type="text/css">
       <!--
7. **P.look** {font-family: arial; font-size:16px;
    color : blue}
8. **P.fonts** { font-size: 20pt; color: maroon;}
9. hr{position: absolute; width:200px; left: 20px }
       -->
10. </style> </HEAD> <BODY>

11. <P class="look">The font 16px underline!
12. </P> <hr>
13. <P class="fonts">The font 20px Maroon!
    </P>
14. </BODY>
15. </HTML>

It recalls the classes that we are already called *look* and *fonts*. It produces different color text.

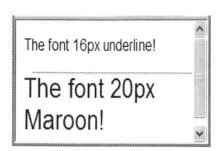

Note: We put the CSS code inside HTML comment. The above line **<!--** and **-->** is NOT a comment which compiler refuse to validate it but we must use it. Why should we use it? The reality is that some old browsers do not validate the CSS code therefore they output the code itself as a text.

A class can be a dot like ".**words** "Then you can call it inside your code .Checkout this example.

Example: 10.4
1. <!DOCTYPE HTML PUBLIC "-//W3C//DTD HTML 4.01//EN"
2. "http://www.w3.org/TR/html4/Strict.dtd">
3. <head>
4. <meta http-equiv="Content-Type" content="text/html; charset=iso-8859-1">
5. <title> Class Selector</title>
6. <style type="text/css">
7. <!--
8. **.Text**{ font-size:14px;color:blue;}
9. -->
10. </STYLE>
11. </HEAD> <BODY>
12. <P> <SPAN CLASS= Text> Result of the CLASS</SPAN>
13. Out of style!
14. <SPAN STYLE="font-family: Arial; font-size:10px; color: maroon;">
15. This is inline style</SPAN></P>
16. </BODY>
17. </HTML>

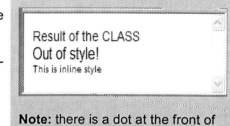

Note: there is a dot at the front of Text on line 8.

ID selector

Another way of using selector is by using ID selector. ID selector is used when you want to call a unique object with its related ID. It is usually used for different layers.

The general syntax for ID selector:

#IDSelector { property : Value ; }

Example: 10.5
1. <!DOCTYPE HTML PUBLIC "-//W3C//DTD HTML 4.01//EN"
2. "http://www.w3.org/TR/html4/Strict.dtd">
3. <head>
4. <meta http-equiv="Content-Type" content="text/html; charset=iso-8859-1">
5. <title> ID Selector</title>
6. <style type="text/css">
7. #ID1 { background-color:yellow; width:25%; }
8. #ID2 { {font-family: arial; }
9. </style>
10. </head> <body>
11. <p id="ID1">Text background = yellow</p>
12. <p id="ID2">font-family=Arial</p>
13. </body>
14. </html>

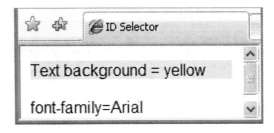

Group Class Selector

You can use grouped class styles which are several classes in one group. These classes are actually the same with only little differences. For example, there could be the same text and the same background color, but the fonts could be different.

.code1 *{font-family : "arial narrow"; color:red; background:blue; font-size:14pt;}*

.code2 *{font-family :"arial narrow"; color:red; background:blue; font-size:18pt;}*
You see that both classes are the same except that their fonts are different in size.

Now we know how to use styles in CSS. Therefore, the remaining CSS lessons will be extremely easy. We will start with formatting text and move on to more advanced features.

Font

CSS font provides different font-weight: font-style and font-family. Just look at this table which shows the different features of files.

Property	Example
font-family	font-family : arial, san-serif
font-size	font-size: normal font-size:10px (pixel size) font-size:12pt (point size) **Relative size :** font-size:small font-size:x-small font-size:xx-small font-size:smaller font-size:medium font-size:large font-size:x-large font-size:xx-large font-size:larger font-size:55%
font-style	font-style:normal font-style:italic font-style:oblique
font-weight	font-weight:normal font-weight:bold font-weight:bolder font-weight:lighter **font-weight:100**
• If the font-family is made up of two parts, like Arial narrow, then you should place it in quotation marks like, font-family: "Arial narrow". • The font-weight can be between 100 and 900. • Normal=400 and bold=700	

Example: 10.6
1. <!DOCTYPE HTML PUBLIC "-//W3C//DTD HTML 4.01//EN"
2. "http://www.w3.org/TR/html4/Strict.dtd">
3. <head>
4. <meta http-equiv="Content-Type" content="text/html; charset=iso-8859-1">
5. <title> CSS Fonts</title>
6. <style type="text/css">
7. <!--
8. span.font1 { font-family: san-serif; font-size: 14px;}

9. span.font2 { font-size: 14pt; font-style: oblique;}
10. span.font3 { font-weight: bolder;}
11. -->
12. </style>
13. </head> <body> <p>
14. <span   class="font1">San-serif,   size
    14px></span>
15. <span class="font2">Style oblique, size
    14pt</span>
16. <span   class="font3">Weight
    bolder</span>
17. </p> </body>
18. </html>

Span and div

We use span in the above example. By themselves, **div** and **span** do not cause any effect. They are, therefore, the best candidates for naming a CSS class. You will see many examples in CSS that use both span and div. The *div* and *span* do not style anything within the code, but we use them as HTML keywords.

Colors

CSS provides the simplest way to create and manipulate colors. Color can be page background, text background and text color. You can use the color name like "**gray**", the color hexadecimal like "**#bebebe**" or the RGB like **rgb(190 190 190)**. All three forms produce the color gray. Unlike HTML, you do not need to create a table in order to use a specific text background with CSS.

Four ways to declare RGB:
- #rrggbb (e.g., #00FF00)
- #rgb (e.g., #0F0)
- rgb(int, int, int) where int is an integer between 0 and 255 like : rgb(10,232,00))
- rgb(X%,X%,X%) where X% is a percentage number between 0.0 and 100: rgb(0%,80%,0%)

Example: 10.7
1. <!DOCTYPE HTML PUBLIC "-//W3C//DTD HTML 4.01//EN"
2. "http://www.w3.org/TR/html4/Strict.dtd">
3. <head>
4. <meta http-equiv="Content-Type" content="text/html; charset=iso-8859-1">
5. <title> Different Backgrounds</title>
6. <style type="text/css">
7. <!--
8. body { background-color: yellow; }
9. div.textBack1 { background-color: gray; width:30%}
10. div.textBack2{ background-color: white; width:30%}

11. div.textColor{ background-color: white; color : #0000ff; width:30% }
12. -->
13. </style> </head> <body>
14. <h3>Yellow Page Background </h3>
15. <div class="textBack2"> <b>
    Background text is in white </b> </div>
16. <div class="textBack1"> <b>
    Background text is in gray! </b> </div>
17. <div class="textColor"><b> White
    background, blue text ! </b> </div>
18. </body>
19. </html>

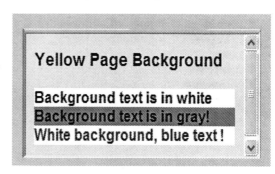

To color text background:	div.textBack1 { background-color: gray; }
Text foreground:	div.textColor{ color: " #0000ff " }
You can use the RGB value:	div.textColor{ color:rgb(0 0 255) }
To color page background:	body { background-color: yellow; }

CSS background
The background can be a solid color set as the RGB, the color name, or the color hexadecimal value. We have already seen the background color in the previous example, **body { background-color: yellow; }**. Now we will work on the background image.

Background image
Background color provides many attributes such as Background-color, Background-image, Background-attachment, Background-repeat and Background-position.

Background names	Attributes
Background-image	url, none
Background-attachment	Fixed, scroll
Background-color	Repeat, repeat-x, repeat-y, no-repeat
Background-position	Percentage(%), pixel, top, bottom, left, right, center

Example: 10.8
1. <!DOCTYPE HTML PUBLIC "-//W3C//DTD HTML 4.01//EN"
2. "http://www.w3.org/TR/html4/Strict.dtd">
3. <head>
4. <meta http-equiv="Content-Type" content="text/html; charset=iso-8859-1">
5. <title> background images</title>
6. <style type="text/css">

7. <!--
8. body {
9. background-image:url('phone.gif') }
10. h3 {background-color:white; }
11. -->
12. </style>
13. </head>
14. <body>
15. <p> </p>
16. </body>
17. </html>

You may want to arrange your background so that lining up in a vertical format. Use **repeat-y;** in order to see the vertical background.
Check out this example.

Example: 10.9
1. <!DOCTYPE HTML PUBLIC "-//W3C//DTD HTML 4.01//EN"
2. "http://www.w3.org/TR/html4/Strict.dtd">
3. <head>
4. <meta http-equiv="Content-Type" content="text/html; charset=iso-8859-1">
5. <title> Vertical Images</title>
6. <style type="text/css">
7. <!--
8. body {
9. background-color: yellow;
10. background-image:url("c:\\pic1.jpg");
11. background-repeat: repeat-y; }
12. h3{text-align:center;}
13. -->
14. </style> </head>
15. <body>
16. <h3> Meidan Azadi
 Vertical Images
    </h3>
17. </body>
18. </html>

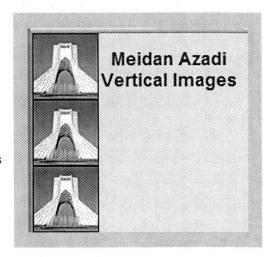

You can simply change **repeat-y** to **repeat-x** in the above example. You will then see the horizontal images.

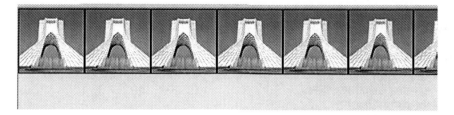

To load an image only once, use the **no-repeat** attribute.

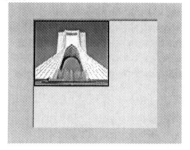

```
body
{
background-color: yellow;
background-image:url('pic1.jpg');
background-repeat: no-repeat;
}
```

To see image in the center, add this line:
background-position: center;
An image can be placed on the left, right, top, bottom, center, and by percentage measures.

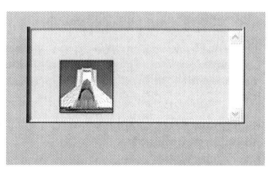

```
body
{
background-color: yellow;
background-image:url('pic1.jpg');
background-repeat: no-repeat;
background-position: 20% 80%;
}
```
It places an image 20% on the X-axis and 80% on the Y-axis.
You can use pixels like: 20px 60px

One interesting attribute is **fixed**. It does not let a loaded image scroll along with the text.

Example: 10.10

```
1. <!DOCTYPE HTML PUBLIC "-//W3C//DTD HTML 4.01//EN"
2. "http://www.w3.org/TR/html4/Strict.dtd">
3. <head>
4. <meta http-equiv="Content-Type" content="text/html; charset=iso-8859-1">
5. <title> Exact position</title>
6. <style type="text/css">
        <!--
7. body  {
8. background-color: yellow;
9. background-image:url('C:\\pic1.jpg');
10. background-repeat: no-repeat;
11. background-position: 10% 10%;
12. background-attachment : fixed;
13. }
        -->
14. </style> </head>
15. <body>
16. <h2>*******************
17. *************************
18. *************************
19. *************************
20. *************************</h2>
21. </body>
22. </html>
```

Try to **minimize** the browser to see the active scroll. Then up and down scrollbar to see only text will move without effecting the image. Now use this code to bring the picture to the center and to stop it from being scrollable:

Body
{
background:url('pic1.jpg')
no-repeat fixed center;
}

Resize background

The background can be resized according to width and height. This can be done by the amount of pixels or percentage. You can also use border thickness and other border attributes which we will discuss later on.

```
div.background  {
 width: 300px;
 height: 200px;
 background: url(c:\\pic1.jpg) repeat;
 border: 2px solid black;
 }
```

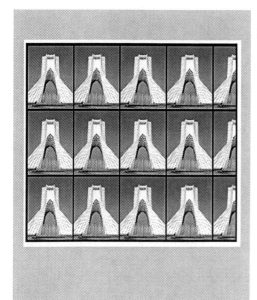

Example: 10.11
1. <!DOCTYPE HTML PUBLIC "-//W3C// DTD HTML 4.01//EN"
2. "http://www.w3.org/TR/html4/Strict.dtd">
3. <head>
4. <meta http-equiv="Content-Type" content ="text/html; charset=iso-8859-1">
5. <title> height, width</title>
6. <style type="text/css">
7. <!--
8. div.background {
9. width: 300px; height: 200px;
10. background: url(c:\\pic1.jpg) repeat;
11. border: 2px solid black; }
12. -->
13. </style> </head> <body>
14. <div class="background"></div>
15. </body>
16. </html>

If the image is not loaded then the border will be shown on the screen. The border can be solid black, as you can see in the example.

CSS comments

Comments are design to describe the code. This feature does not have any effect on the browser. In fact, the browser never reads it. The comment is like this, */* comment */*
For example:
div.background */*class background*/*
{
width: 300px; */*width 300 pixel this just comment*/*
height: 200px;
background: url(c:\\pic1.jpg) repeat;

Review questions
1- Why CSS
2- What is the selector?
3- Write the general syntax for CSS selector.
4- Write a statement to display an image as the background.
5- Write a statement to control the image position.
6- Give an example of font size and style.
7- Write a statement to control the image (NOT MOVE WITH TEXT).
8- Fix this statement **div.textColor{ colors : grb(10 10 255) }**
9- What is inline style in CSS?
10- How do you set a background width and height?

Answers
1- To develop web page and help HTML code.
2- The selector is essential to the CSS code; we declare it and then use it in the body of the code.
3- Selector{property: value;}
4- Background :url(path)
5- **background-position: center;**
6- Font-size: 14pt; font-style:normal;
7- background-attachment: fixed;
8- **div.textColor{ color : rgb(10 10 255) }**
9- You directly change color, fonts and so on, anywhere inside your code.
10- div.background

```
{
width: 300px;
height: 200px;
background: url(c:\\pic1.jpg) repeat;
border: 2px solid black;
}
```

Chapter 11

Formatting text in CSS

- Introduction
- CSS border
- Text properties
- Margin
- Padding
- CSS lists
- Different list shapes
- CSS table
- Simple table
- Alternative colors
- Managing table
- Laboratory exercises

Introduction

CSS provides great formatting features for text. You can simply set your style within the head and use your per-styles within the HTML code. It is interesting to know that with CSS you can create tables that look like image graphics. Through the manipulation of the border, color, padding and so on, the borders and cells of object can be really attractive. You can easily change the margin, space and height of the font to your desired format. In this chapter we try to bring the most attractive features of CSS.

First we must continue the topics from the last chapter. Here we look at the CSS border.

CSS border

CSS is enriched in border attributes used to manipulate the border. In many cases, the combination of different border attributes makes a difference. The webpage must use a border that is related to the content of the page.

Properties	Values	Example
border-bottom-width **border-left-width** **border-width** **border-top-width** **border-right-width**	thin, medium, thick, length	border-bottom-width: thin
border-top-color **border-right-color** **border-bottom-color** **border-left-color** **border-color**	Any color, Use RGB, color name or hexadecimal value	border-right-color: blue or border-bottom-color: #CCCCCC
border-bottom-style **border-left-style** **border-style** **border-top-style** **border-right-style**	none, solid, double, groove, ridge, inset, outset You can use a combination of several attributes.	border-right-style: groove border-style: dotted border-style: hidden border-style: solid
border-top **border-right** **border-bottom** **border-left** **border**	*border-width ,border-style , border-color*	border-bottom: thick inset yellow

This example shows the different types of border design. You can design various borders with CSS border attributes.

Example: 11.1

```
1.  <!DOCTYPE HTML PUBLIC "-//W3C//DTD HTML 4.01//EN"
2.  "http://www.w3.org/TR/html4/Strict.dtd">
3.  <head>
4.  <meta http-equiv="Content-Type" content="text/html; charset=iso-8859-1">
5.  <title> CSS Borders</title>
6.  <style type="text/css">
7.  <!--
8.  p.solid {border-style: solid; border-top:
    thin blue dashed;}
9.  p.dot {border-style: dotted}
10. p.rid {border-style: ridge; }
11. p.grv {border-style: groove }
12. p.dash {border-style: dashed; }
13. p.inset {border-style: inset; }
14. p.outset {border-style: outset; }
15. p.sdouble {border-style: solid
    double;border-width:15px}
16. -->
17. </style> </head> <body>
18. <p class="solid"> SOLID top dashed!
    </p>
19. <p class="dot">DOTTED</p>
20. <p class="rid">RIDGE</p>
21. <p class="grv">GROOVE</p>
22. <p class="dash">DASHED</p>
23. <p class="inset">INSET</p>
24. <p class="outset">OUTSET</p>
25. <p class="sdouble">SOLID
    DOUBLE</p>
26. </body>
27. </html>
```

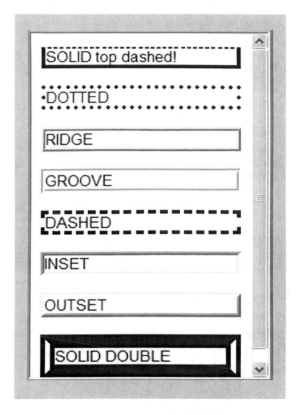

Various combinations of colors, styles and size can make an appealing image on the screen. Here we will try to put them together in order to create a picture frame.

Example: 11.2

```
1.  <!DOCTYPE HTML PUBLIC "-//W3C//DTD HTML 4.01//EN"
2.  "http://www.w3.org/TR/html4/Strict.dtd">
3.  <head>
4.  <meta http-equiv="Content-Type" content="text/html; charset=iso-8859-1">
5.  <title> Fancy Border</title>
6.  <style type="text/css">
        <!--
7.  div {
8.  border-left-style: ridge;
```

```
9. border-left-color: maroon;
10.border-left-width: 30px;
11.border-bottom-style: ridge;
12.border-bottom-color: yellow;
13.border-bottom-width: 30px;
14.border-right-style: ridge;
15.border-right-color: maroon;
16.border-right-width: 30px;
17.border-top-style: ridge;
18.border-top-color: yellow;
19.border-top-width: 30px;
20.}
        -->
21.</style></head> <body>
22.<h2>CSS Borders</h2>
23.<div><b>Nice border on screen!</b></div>
24.</body>
25.</html>
```

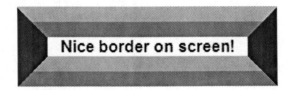

Text properties

There are many text properties that help us to design text inside the webpage. We will cover most of them in some easy to understand examples.

Look at some of the basic text properties.

Properties	Value	Example
letter-spacing	Normal, *length*	letter-spacing:4pt
vertical-align	Sub, super	vertical-align:sub
text-decoration	none, underline, overline, line-through	text-decoration:none
text-transform	capitalize, uppercase, lowercase, none	text-transform: lowercase
text-align	left, right, center, justify	text-align: center
text-indent	*Length, percentage*	text-indent:10px
line-height	normal, *number*, *length*, *percentage*	line-height:normal
white-space	normal, pre, nowrap	White-space:normal

Letter-spacing causes some spaces between characters. You can use pixels to manage these spaces. Text-transform can change whole texts to "capitalize format", in which every letter of the first word will be capitalized.

Example: 11.3
1. <!DOCTYPE HTML PUBLIC "-//W3C//DTD HTML 4.01//EN"
2. "http://www.w3.org/TR/html4/Strict.dtd">
3. <head>
4. <meta http-equiv="Content-Type" content="text/html; charset=iso-8859-1">
5. <title> Formatting Text</title>
6. <style type="text/css">
7. <!--
8. div.space1 {letter-spacing: 1px} div.space2{letter-spacing: 0.2cm}
9. div.transform{text-transform:capitalize}
10. div.height{line-height:300%}
11. -->
12. </style> </head> <body> <div>
13. <div class="space1">Character spaces at 5px</div>
14. <div class="space2">Character spaces at 0.2cm </div>
15. <div class="transform">text is capitalized</div>
16. <div class="height">Line height is 300</div>
17. </div> </body> </html>

Character spaces at 5px
C h a r a c t e r   s p a c e s   a t   0 . 2 c m
T e x t   I s   C a p i t a l i z e d

L i n e   H e i g h t   I s   3 0 0

Margin

Margin helps to place a text onto the page. It provides four attribute sides: right, left, bottom and top. Each side can be measured by px or pt.

Margin Properties		
Properties	**Value**	**Example**
margin-top	*length, percentage,* auto	margin-top:5px
margin-bottom		margin-bottom:5em
margin-left		margin-left:5pt
margin-right		margin-right:5px
margin		margin:15px 5px 10px 15px

If you want to use four values, you can use four values like {margin: 5px 5px 5px 5px} more simply than top, bottom, left and right.

- First value = top
- Second value = right
- Third value = bottom
- Forth value = left

If you only use two values, they will be the top and bottom:
{margin: 5px 5px } This means Top=5px bottom=5px

Example: 11.4

```
1.   <!DOCTYPE HTML PUBLIC "-//W3C//DTD HTML 4.01//EN"
2.   "http://www.w3.org/TR/html4/Strict.dtd">
3.   <head>
4.   <meta http-equiv="Content-Type" content="text/html; charset=iso-8859-1">
5.   <title> Text Margin</title>
6.   <style type="text/css">
7.   <!--
8.   <style type="text/css">
9.   div.Margin1{margin-right: 20px;
10.  margin-top:5px;
11.  margin-bottom: 10px;  margin-left: 0px;
12.  border: thin black dashed; }
13.  div.Margin2{margin-right: 20px;
14.  margin-top:20px;  margin-bottom: 0px;
15.  margin-left: 100px;  border: 5px dashed; }
16.  div.Margin3{margin:10px 10px 10px 10px ;
17.  border: 5px solid red; }
18.  -->
19.  </style> </head> <body>
20.  <div>
21.  <div class="Margin1">The text left margin is: 0 </div>
22.  <div class="Margin2">The text left margin is:100</div>
23.  <div class="Margin3">The text left margin is:10</div>
24.  </div> </body> </html>
```

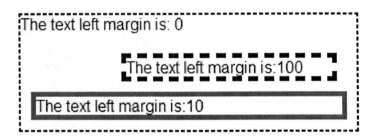

Note: We use border along with margin to show the margin on the screen. In fact, just look at the border to see how far away it is placed from the main border.

Padding

CSS padding is like the CSS margin except that there is white space between margins or between actual contents.

padding-top, padding-right, padding-bottom, and padding-left.

For example:

p { padding: 5px 5px 5px 5px; }

The **BOX MODLING** has five properties:

- height
- width
- margin
- border
- padding

Padding properties (box)		
Property	**Value**	**Example**
padding-top	*length, percentage*	**padding-top:12%**
padding-bottom		**padding-bottom: 2em**
padding-right		**padding-right:15px**
padding-left		**padding-left:15pt; }**
padding	Four value	**padding: 10px 5px 12px 15px**

Example: 11.5

1. `<!DOCTYPE HTML PUBLIC "-//W3C//DTD HTML 4.01//EN"`
2. `"http://www.w3.org/TR/html4/Strict.dtd">`
3. `<head>`
4. `<meta http-equiv="Content-Type" content="text/html; charset=iso-8859-1">`
5. `<title> Padding</title>`
6. `<style type="text/css">`
7. `<!--`
8. `div.border{border:5px dashed; width:50%} /*5px from every edges*/`
9. `div.padd {`
10. `background-color:yellow;`
11. `padding:10px;   /*size of padding*/`
12. `margin:20px; }       /*Margin 20px from border*/`
13. `-->`
14. `</style> </head> <body>`
15. `<div class="border">`
16. `<div class="padd">Padding is set to 10px, Border, Margin, Padding.</div>`
17. `</div> </body>`
18. `</html>`

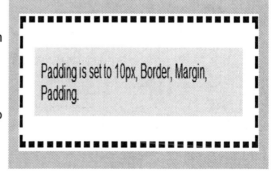

You can see that the border is in a dashed line. You can also see a margin between the border and the padding. The last one is in yellow, indicating an area of padding.
On line 9 you will see **margin: 20px**, meaning that the margin is set to be 10 pixels in all directions (*top=20px, bottom=20px, right=20px, left=20px*).

CSS lists

A CSS list provides a wide variety of options. In addition to the many attributes, you can attach your own bullet to the list. Look at some properties that are listed here.

List Properties

Property	Value	Example
list-style-position	inside outside	ol { list-style-position:inside; } ul { list-style-position:outside; }
list-style-image	URL	ul { list-style-image:url(image1.jpg); }
list-style	Can declare multiple attributes list-style-type list-style-position list-style-image	ul { list-style:disc inside url(image.gif); }
marker-offset	auto	ol:before { display:marker; marker-offset:3px; }
list-style-type	disc, circle, square decimal decimal-leading-zero lower-roman upper-roman lower-alpha upper-alpha lower-greek lower-latin upper-latin hebrew armenian georgian cjk-ideographic hiragana katakana hiragana-iroha katakana-iroha	ol { list-style-type: lower-latin; } ul { list-style-type:circle; }

Different list shapes

In this example you will see a circle shape, square shape, disc shape and a bullet shape. The bullet is attached by reading from the image file. The **bul1.gif** is the image file that exists in the folder and we can simply call it.

Example: 11.6

```
1.  <!DOCTYPE HTML PUBLIC "-//W3C//DTD HTML 4.01//EN"
2.  "http://www.w3.org/TR/html4/Strict.dtd">
3.  <head>
4.  <meta http-equiv="Content-Type" content="text/html; charset=iso-8859-1">
5.  <title> CSS List</title>
6.  <style type="text/css">
7.  <!--
8.  ul.disc {list-style-type: disc}
9.  ul.circle {list-style-type: circle}
10. ul.square {list-style-type: square}
11. ul.image{ list-style-image:url(c:\\bul1.gif);}
12. -->
13. </style> </head> <body>
14. <ul class="disc"><li> Bananas</li></ul>
15. <ul class="circle"><li> Grapes </li></ul>
16. <ul class="square"><li> Apples </li></ul>
17. <ul class="image"><li> Oranges </li></ul>
18. </body>
19. </html>
```

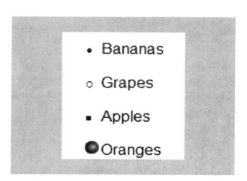

You can use such features as background, margin and padding along with the list. In this example we use a table in order to show the different list attributes.

Example: 11.7

1. <!DOCTYPE HTML PUBLIC "-//W3C// DTD HTML 4.01//EN"
2. "http://www.w3.org/ TR/html4/Strict.dtd">
3. <head>
4. <meta http-equiv= "Content-Type" content ="text/html; charset=iso-8859-1">
5. <title> Different List Styles</title>
6. <style type="text/css">
7. <!--
8. ul.disc {list-style-type: disc}
9. ol.list1 {
10. list-style-type: circle; }
11. ol.list2 { list-style-type: square; }
12. ol.list3 { list-style-type: upper-roman;}
13. ol.list4 {list-style-image: url(arrow.gif);}
14. -->
15. </style> </head>
16. <body>
17. <table border=1>
18. <tr> <td>
19. <ol class="list1">
20. <li> Red</li> <li> Blue </li>
21. <li> Yellow</li> </ol> </td>
22. <td><ol class="list2">
23. <li> Red</li> <li> Blue </li> <li> Yellow</li></ol></td>
24. <td><ol class="list3">
25. <li> Red</li> <li> Blue </li> <li> Yellow</li></ol></td>
26. <td><ol class="list4">
27. <li> Red</li> <li> Blue </li> <li> Yellow</li></ol></td>
28. </tr> </table>
29. </body> </html>

▶The arrow in the out is obtained from a file. The image file is called **arrow.gif**. You can download any thumbnail image and use it within the list.

o Red	■ Red	I. Red	▸ Red
o Blue	■ Blue	II. Blue	▸ Blue
o Yellow	■ Yellow	III. Yellow	▸ Yellow

CSS table

A table is a way of displaying data. When you want to display data on screen, you need some form of tabular format. Many programmers make different designs and layouts for their tables. CSS provides sufficient properties to format a table according to data needs. Use the <table>, <TR>,<TD> and <TH>tags to build your table.
Use the <caption> tag to create caption for the table.
<caption> *This is a simple table*</caption>
Use the <TH> tag to format your header:
TH { text-align: center; font-weight: bold }

Table Properties in CSS

Property	Value
border-collapse	collapse separate
border-spacing	length length
caption-side	top bottom left right
empty-cell	show hide
table-layout	auto fixed

Simple table

The table-layout determines how a table should be laid out. It can be automatic or fixed. If you use a fixed cell then it does not stretch along with the data size.

table-layout: automatic

table-layout: fixed

You can set the height and width of the cell.

Example: 11.8

```
1. <!DOCTYPE HTML PUBLIC "-//W3C//DTD HTML 4.01//EN"
2. "http://www.w3.org/TR/html4/Strict.dtd">
3. <head>
4. <meta http-equiv="Content-Type" content="text/html; charset=iso-8859-1">
5. <title> Basic Table in CSS</title>
6. <style type="text/css">
7. <!--
8. table.format1 {
9. table-layout: automatic
10.}
11.table.format2 {table-layout:fixed  }
12.-->
13.</style></head><body>
14.<table class="format1" border="1" width="100%">
15.<caption> This is an automatic table</caption>
16.<tr> <td>This automatic cell handles a large size of data</td>
17.<td width="70%">This automatic cell handles a large size of data</td>
18.</tr> </table>
19.<table class="format2" border="1" width="100%">
20.<caption>This is a fixed cell</caption>
21.<tr><td>This automatic cell handles a large size of data</td>
22.<td>This automatic cell handles a large size of data</td>
23.</tr></table></body> </html>
```

This is an automatic table

This automatic cell handles a large size of data	This automatic cell handles a large size of data

This is a fixed cell

This automatic cell handles a large size of data	This automatic cell handles a large size of data

Alternative colors

We can color each cell alternatively with CSS. For example, we can have the first row in yellow and the second row in white. The third row will automatically will be in yellow again and the pattern will continue.

Example: 11.9

1. <!DOCTYPE HTML PUBLIC "-//W3C//DTD HTML 4.01//EN"
2. "http://www.w3.org/TR/html4/Strict.dtd">
3. <head>
4. <meta http-equiv="Content-Type" content="text/html; charset=iso-8859-1">
5. <title> Alternative color</title>
6. <style type="text/css">
7. <!--
8. tr.ALT1 td {
9. background-color: #FC0; color: black; }
10. tr.ALT2 td {
11. background-color: #99FFCC; color: rgb(0,0,0); }
12. -->
13. </style></head>
14. <body><table>
15. <tr class="ALT1"> <td>Rent </td>
    <td>$679</td></tr>
16. <tr class="ALT2"><td>Telephone </td>
    <td>$46.95</td> </tr>
17. <tr class="ALT1"> <td>Hydro</td> <td>$125.55
    </td> </tr>
18. <tr class="ALT2"> <td>Internet </td>
    <td>$46.25</td></tr>
19. </table> </body>
20. </html>

Rent	$679
Telephone	$46.95
Hydro	$125.55
Internrt	$46.25

Managing table
A CSS table can have a better look and display data in an effective way.

Example: 11.10

```
1.  <!DOCTYPE HTML PUBLIC "-//W3C//DTD HTML 4.01//EN"
2.  "http://www.w3.org/TR/html4/Strict.dtd">
3.  <head>
4.  <meta http-equiv="Content-Type" content="text/html; charset=iso-8859-1">
5.  <title> Design Nice  Table</title>
6.  <style type="text/css">
7.  <!--
8.  table {background: blue; border: 10px ridge yellow; margin: 10px; }
9.  TD {
10. background: white; border: outset 5pt; vertical-align: right;
11. padding: 14px; }
12. CAPTION {
13. border-left-style: ridge; border-left-color: yellow; border-left-width: 10px;
14. border-bottom-style: ridge;
15. border-bottom-color: yellow;
16. border-bottom-width: 10px;
17. border-right-style: ridge;
18. border-right-color: yellow;
19. border-right-width: 10px;
20. border-top-style: ridge;
21. border-top-color: yellow;
22. border-top-width: 10px;
23. }
24. -->
25. </style></head>
26. <body>
27. <table>
28. <caption>Students Expenses Amount</caption>
29. <tfoot><tr>
30. <td colspan="2">Total Amounts: 4851.50</td>
31. </tr></tfoot>
32. <tbody><tr>
33. <td>Fall Expenses</td>
34. <td>$1500.00</td>
35. </tr><tr>
36. <td>Winter Expenses</td>
37. <td>$1700.55.00</td>
38. </tr><tr>
39. <td>Spring Expenses</td>
40. <td>$1650.95</td>
41. </tr></tbody>
42. </table></body></HTML>
```

Students Expenses Amount	
Fall Expenses	$1500.00
Winter Expenses	$1700.55.00
Spring Expenses	$1650.95
Total Amounts: 4851.50	

The CAPTION, which starts from line 14 and continues to line 31, is written to create a nice caption with a ridge of yellow color. This frame has already been seen in this chapter. Change <tfoot></tfoot> to <thead></thead> on line 32 and observe the result.

Students Expenses Amount	
Total Amounts: 4851.50	
Fall Expenses	$1500.00
Winter Expenses	$1700.55.00
Spring Expenses	$1650.95

Laboratory exercises

1-With the power of CSS, create a layout that divides a page into three potions.

    1-   Top Header (20% width): Set the company logo

    2-   Left (20%): Place for the site navigation

    3-   Right (80%): The main site.

2- Create the table and design it with CSS attributes. The design depends on your artistic abilities. The table must be floatable. This means that it enlarges as the caption gets bigger.

Chapter 12

Link and image effects

- Introduction
- CSS Link
- CSS text decoration
- Mouse activation
- Link decoration
- Cursor manipulation
- Overflow
- Creating external CCS
- Linking external CSS file
- CSS Multi-page headers
- Positioning Images
- Shadow position effect
- Alpha effect
- Blur effect
- FlipH & FlipV
- Wave effect
- More effects
- Laboratory exercises

Introduction

We have already seen the impact of linage in the parts of this book that refer to HTML. CSS (Cascading Style Sheets) has magnificent features that allow us to work with the link and implement the images. In this chapter we will learn about all the important aspects of CSS and we will demonstrate interesting mouse shapes and mouse behavior. We will demonstrate how to work with images, which prior to CSS we had to do with graphics.

CSS Link

Link in CSS facilitates the page linkage. There are four selectors:
- A:link
- A:visited
- A:active
- A:hover

A:link is used for a new link.
A:visited is used for a visited link.
A:active is used for an activate the link when you click on it.
A:hover is used for when the mouse hovers over the link (e.g. changes color).

Example: 12.1
1.   <!DOCTYPE HTML PUBLIC "-//W3C//DTD HTML 4.01//EN"
2.   "http://www.w3.org/TR/html4/Strict.dtd">
3.   <head>
4.   <meta http-equiv="Content-Type" content="text/html; charset=iso-8859-1">
5.   <title> Link</title>
6.   <style type="text/css">
7.   <!--
8.   body{background-color: yellow;}
9.   -->
10.   </style> </head> <body>
11.   <p> <a href="http://www.yahoo.com"> Visit Yahoo Site</a>
12.   </p> </body> </html>

Visit Yahoo Site

This is a simple link. If you click on this link, it goes to the yahoo site. Now, there is a little problem on the above link: You can see that there is a little unwanted bar under the "*Visit Yahoo Site*". To get rid of this bar you need the CSS **text-decoration** selector.

CSS text decoration

Usually we use text decoration along with the CSS link. If the "*text-decoration: none*" attribute is set, then there will not be any bar under the link.

CSS Text-Decoration Properties		
Properties	**Values**	**Example**
text-decoration	*none* *underline* *overline* *line-through* *blink (not supported in IE>*	text-decoration:none text-decoration:underline text-decoration:overline text-decoration:line-through text-decoration:blink

text-decoration:none means that there will not be any decoration around the selected text

text-decoration:underline returns an underline bar

text-decoration:overline returns an over line bar

text-decoration:line-through returns a bar through the text

text-decoration:blink returns blinking but does not work under **IE**

Mouse activation

In this example, simply place the mouse over the link and do not click. You will see it change from **overline** to **underline** and the background will become yellow.

Place mouse over link, don't click!

See Yahoo Engin

By placing the mouse on the link, the bar moves on the top of the link and the background becomes yellow.

Place mouse over link, don't click!

See Yahoo Engin

Example: 12.2

1. <!DOCTYPE HTML PUBLIC "-//W3C//DTD HTML 4.01//EN"
2. "http://www.w3.org/TR/html4/Strict.dtd">
3. <head>
4. <meta http-equiv="Content-Type" content= "text/html; charset=iso-8859-1">
5. <title> Link Decoration</title>
6. <style type="text/css">
7. <!--
8. <head> <style type="text/css">
9. .decore A:link {text-decoration: none}
10. .decore A:visited {text-decoration: none}
11. .decore A:active {text-decoration: overline}
12. .decore A:hover {text-decoration: underline; background-color:yellow; color: balck;}
13. -->
14. </style> </head> <body>
15. <h3> Place mouse over link, don't click! </h3>
16. <div class="decore">
17. <a href="http://www.yahoo.com">See Yahoo Engine </a>
18. </div> </body>
19. </html>

Link decoration

Here you can see another example where mouse-over causes bigger font, overline, underline and background color effects.

decore A:link {text-decoration: none}
.decore A:visited {text-decoration:none; color:black; font-size:15pt}
.decore A:active {text-decoration: none}
.decore A:hover {text-decoration: underline overline; background-color:yellow; color: maroon;font-size:25pt}

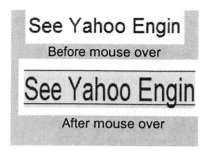

See Yahoo Engin

Before mouse over

See Yahoo Engin

After mouse over

Cursor manipulation

The shape of the cursor can have different indications. For example, when the cursor looks like this shape ⧗ , we understand that we have to wait. When the shape becomes like this shape Ⓚ? , we know that this means help. To use the relevant cursor shape, use this style: **Shape1 {cursor:help}** (this produces the help shape.)

We put the most important shapes in action in this example.

Shape	Name	Shape	Name	Shape	Name
⌖	default	Ⓚ?	help	⇐	w-resize
+	crosshair	⇧	n-resize	⌖	nw-resize
☞	hand	⬀	ne-resize	⌖⧗	progress
☞	pointer	⇒	e-resize	⊘	not-allowed
✜	move	⬂	se-resize	☞⊘	no-drop
I	text	⬇	s-resize	⊢⊣	vertical-text
⧗	wait	⬃	sw-resize	⬌⬍	all-scroll
↔	col-resize	⇕	row-resize	▲	url

Example: 12.3
1. <!DOCTYPE HTML PUBLIC "-//W3C//DTD HTML 4.01//EN"
2. "http://www.w3.org/TR/html4/Strict.dtd">
3. <head>

4. <meta http-equiv="Content-Type" content="text/html; charset=iso-8859-1">
5. <title> Cursor Shapes</title>
6. <style type="text/css">
7. <!--
8. A{text-decoration:none}
9. .hand {cursor:HAND;}
10..help{cursor:HELP;}
11..move{cursor:MOVE;}
12..wait{cursor:WAIT;}
13..all{cursor:all-scroll;}
14..not{cursor:not-allowed;}
        a.   -->
15.</style></head><body> <p><b>
16.<a href="" class="hand"> HAND</a>
17.<a href="" class="help"> HELP </a>
18.<a href="" class= "move"> MOVE</a>
19.<a href="" class="wait">WAIT</a>
20.<a href="" class="all">ALL-SCROLL </a>
21.<a href="" class="not">NOT-ALLOWED </a>
22.</b></p>
23.</body> </html>

```
HAND
HELP
MOVE
WAIT
ALL-SCROLL
NOT-ALLOWED
```

The above example produces cursor shapes. Just place your mouse on the link to see the shape of the cursor.

Overflow

Sometimes you need to use overflow text in order to occupy less spaces. The overflow property is as follows:

Overflow properties	
Visible	Default
Hidden	Does not display scrollbar
Auto	Automatic display of scroll when text is large
Scroll	Display scrollbar

Example: 12.4
1. <!DOCTYPE HTML PUBLIC "-//W3C//DTD HTML 4.01//EN"
2. "http://www.w3.org/TR/html4/Strict.dtd">
3. <head>
4. <meta http-equiv="Content-Type" content="text/html; charset=iso-8859-1">
5. <title> Text overflow</title>
6. <style type="text/css">
7. <!--
8. .overflow {
9. background-color:yellow;

10. text-align:justify; width:140px;
11. height:120px; overflow: scroll }
12. -->
13. </style></head><body>
14. <H5>The overflow scrollbar!</H5>
15. <div class="overflow">
16. We can control the large text to overflow into a little box. It does not occupy a large space!
17. </div></body></html>

The overflow scrollbar!

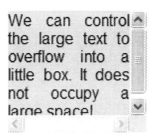

On line 7, the **text-align:justify;** is used justify the text to the right and the left equally. If you set the **overflow:scroll** to **overflow:hidden** on line 10, then you will see that this image has no scrollbar.

we can control the large text to be overflown in a little box. It dose not occupy some large space!

Creating external CCS

Up until now we have worked with internal styles, or the inline style. Now we must see how the external style works. Why do we need to create an external file in CSS? Well, sometimes we need to create a styled file and use it in several pages. For example, if you want your logo, along with the desired colors and fonts, to be repeatedly displayed on the top of each page, you only need to create it once. You simply call it whenever you want it to reappear. Creating a CSS style sheet file is easy. Open your Notepad or any text editor, type your code in CSS format and save the file as **anyName.css**. Remember that the file must be saved with a **css** extension and NOT with an html extension.

Since your file must be saved with a css extension, you do not need to include the **<style type="text/css">** tag.

Linking external CSS file

To link the external style sheet you just put the linkage code inside the page. Where should the code be placed? It should be placed between the <head> and the </head> tags. You could create a style sheet file, call it **design.css,** and then put this code inside the head tag of each page.

```
<HEAD>
<link rel="stylesheet" type="text/css" href="design.css">
</HEAD>
```

Steps to create CSS files

1- Open your text-editor (*Notepad*) and type this code:

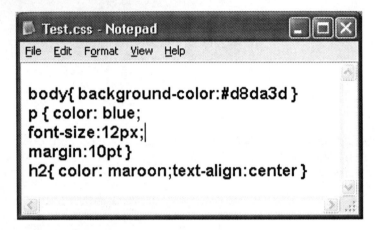

2- Save it as **Test.css** and close this file.
3- Again, open another blank Notepad and type this code:

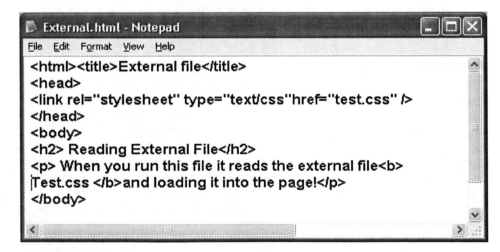

4- Save it as **External.html** then try to run this file (under Windows Explorer, double click on External.html>)

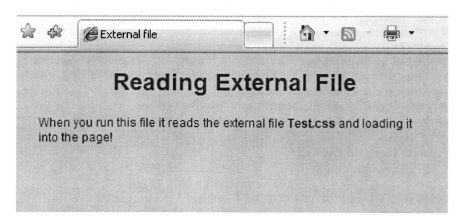

Using the external file can be very beneficial. First, if you want to change something in the design, you do not need to change the code for every single page. Once a change is made in the file, Test.css, it will automatically affect all the pages that call this file. The code also becomes very small and runs faster.

The **<LINK>** tag inside the head, assigned to media type-text/css, is a linking document. If the browser does not support it then the browser ignores it. The LINK tag takes **media** option as follows:
<LINK REL=StyleSheet HREF="myfile.css" TYPE="text/css"
 Style" **MEDIA**="screen">

• **Screen**: default value
• **Print**: for printer
• **Aural**: for speech
• **Braille**: for Braille
• **Tv**: for television
• **All**: for all output devices

You can use multi-declarations such as,
*<LINK REL=StyleSheet HREF="myfile.css" TYPE="text/css"
Style" MEDIA="screen, print">*

The REL specifies the CSS file in the HTML file. It can be used as **alternative**.
*<LINK REL=Alternate StyleSheet HREF="Test.css" TYPE="text/css"
Style" MEDIA="screen, print">*

Alternate means that if the preferred file is not loaded in the page then it uses the alternative file.

CSS Multi-page headers

Sometimes you might need one header for all the pages. You might also create a nice header for all the pages but want the topics inside the header to be different. Once you create the styles, you can use them many times. In this example we will create a header for all of the html pages and we will call that header to be displayed on the top of each page. It is so easy to have several files and it is a good way to always save your program code into different files. First you just save your CSS design as a file with **.css** extension like (myfile.css) then call this file in your html file.

<link rel="stylesheet" type="text/css"href="mufile.css">

Watch this file. I save this file as **style.css** in fact it is just one line code.

```
<!--
body{color:red; font-size:40px;}
-->
```

The *comment* part is an option you can use it or not.
Then I call the **style.css** into my html file. Here is my html file that I save it as **Seelt.html**.

```
<!DOCTYPE HTML PUBLIC "-//W3C//DTD HTML 4.01//EN"
"http://www.w3.org/TR/html4/Strict.dtd">
 <head>
 <meta http-equiv="Content-Type" content="text/html; charset=iso-8859-1">
<title>Image Border Effect</title>
<link rel="stylesheet" type="text/css"href="d1.css">
 </style>  </head> <body>
<p>
Welcome
</p>
</body>
</HTML>
```

After run the **Seelt.html**, it produces this result with font=40px and color- red.

Welcome

Here you have three files. All files must be saved in the same directory; you need to give the exact path if you save it in a different directory.

#1 Save this decoration file as: **header.css**

```
body {background:#FFCC00;}
div {
background: #d8da3d;   border: outset 5pt;
padding: 14px;
font-family:forte, arial;   font-size:20pt;
font-weight:bold;   text-align: center;
border-left-style: ridge;   border-left-color: yellow;
border-left-width: 10px;  border-bottom-style: ridge;
border-bottom-color: yellow; border-bottom-width: 10px;
border-right-style: ridge; border-right-color: yellow;
border-right-width: 10px; border-top-style: ridge;
border-top-color: yellow; border-top-width: 10px;
}
```

#2 save this file as: **Page1.html**

```
1.   <!DOCTYPE HTML PUBLIC "-//W3C//DTD HTML 4.01//EN"
2.   "http://www.w3.org/TR/html4/Strict.dtd">
3.   <head>
4.   <meta http-equiv="Content-Type" content="text/html; charset=iso-8859-1">
5.   <title> CSS Design</title>
6.   <link rel="stylesheet" type="text/css"href="header.css">
7.   </style>
8.   </head>
9.   <body>
10.  <div>Welcome to CSS Technologia</div>
11.  <H3>Introduction to CSS</h3>
12.  <p>
13.  <a href="page2.html"> See Next Page</a>
14.  </p>
15.  </body>
16.  </html>
```

#3 Save this file as: **Page2.html**

```
<html><title>External file Page2</title>
<head>
<link rel="stylesheet" type="text/css"href="header.css" />
</head>
<body>
<div>Advanced Topics In CSS</div>
<H3><center> Advanced CSS Chapter</center></h3>
<a href="page1.html"> <center>Back to Page1</center></a>
</body>
</html>
```

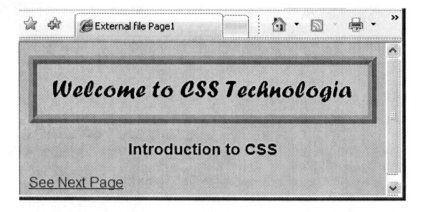

Click on the link "**See Next Page**". You will see the same frame header but it will have different text.

Try to add *absolute positions* to your decoration file (**header.css**), and then run your file.
    position: absolute;
    width:80%;
    margin-top:1em;

margin-left:10%;

▐► **Note:** For simplicity we put CSS and HTML into the same file, but you can put them into several different files.

Positioning Images

There are many great ways to manipulate images, text and other aspects of a web page with CSS. Resizing an image is possible by using **height** and **width**. The position of an image can be relative or absolute. Filter is a very interesting feature of CSS. The filter lets us play around with the image without having to use any particular graphics software.

▐► **Note:** Filter works on the text that height and width has defined.

Filter name	Effect
Filter: alpha	Creates opacity that becomes light by the end
Filter: blur	Creates blurred object
Filter: chroma	Works with image, makes image transparent
Filter: dropshadow	Creates dropping shadow along X and y with specified color
Filter: glow	Creates some glow around the object
Filter: shadow	Something between dropshadow and glow
Filter: flipH	Flipping horizontally
Filter: flipV	Flipping vertically
Filter: grayscale	Converts color to shaded gray
Filter: wave	Creates wave shapes with an object
Filter: xray	Grayscale color, similar to a x-ray image
Filter: invert	Creates the negative or opposite site of the color number
Filter: mask	Shifts from transparent to specified color

CSS positions can be...
- Relative: using properties ratite(X), top, bottom, right and left.
- Fixed: the same absolute except the parent will be the browser.
- Absolute: the real, absolute given position.
- Static: the default option all elements will be in during normal flow.

Example: 12.5

```
1. <!DOCTYPE HTML PUBLIC "-//W3C//DTD HTML 4.01//EN"
2. "http://www.w3.org/TR/html4/Strict.dtd">
3. <head>
4. <meta http-equiv="Content-Type" content="text/html; charset=iso-8859-1">
5. <title>CSS Shadows</title>
6. <style type="text/css">
7. <!--
8. span {
9. display:inline-block; width:350; height:30;
10.font-size:30px; font-family:arial;
11.color:#000000; font-weight:bold;
12.filter:shadow(color=#daa520,direction=225)
13.}
14.img{
15.position: relative;
16.width:100px; height:70px;
17.left:10px; top:10px
18.filter:shadow(color=#daa520,
   direction=225)
19.-->
20.</style> </head> <body> <p>
21.<img src="C:\\dog.jpg" ALT=
   "Shadowing an image!"> <br>
22.<span> Text in Shadow</span>
23.</p> </body>
24.</HTML>
```

▶ **Note:** in Internet Explorer (IE) use **display:inline-block;** otherwise you may not get the exact result.

You can see the pleasing effect without using any graphical application. Both the text and the image are shadowed by 225. The 225 is the default effect. Here, we will try to examine more CSS effects.

Shadow position effect

The shadow position effect is quit simple. It works **clockwise**, with the zero on the top of the page and 180 at the bottom.

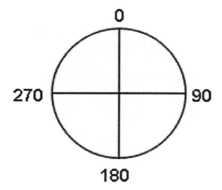

0 = Top
90 = Right
180 = Bottom
225 = Bottom left is
the default option
270 = Left

The 45 is top right, the 320 is top left, and so on.
On line 9 the color is set to #000000, which means black (text color).
The shadow takes two values: the shadow color and the direction.

Alpha effect

Make object blend.
Opacity can be from zero (transparent) to 100 (fully opaque).
Style makes the shape of opacity, such as with the following:
0 = uniform
1 = linear
2 = radial
3 = rectangular
StartX and **startY** means begin on X and Y. On the other hand, the **finishX** and **finishY**
mean the end which is oppose the start.

Example: 12.6
1. <!DOCTYPE HTML PUBLIC "-//W3C//DTD HTML 4.01//EN"
2. "http://www.w3.org/TR/html4/Strict.dtd">
3. <head>
4. <meta http-equiv="Content-Type" content="text/html; charset=iso-8859-1">
5. <title>Alpha</title>
6. <style type="text/css">
7. <!--
8. span
9. {
10. display:inline-block;
11. width:250; height:30; font-size:30px;
12. font-family:arial; color:# 000000;
13. font-weight:bold;
14. filter:alpha(Opacity=80,   FinishOpacity=10, Style=3,
15. StartX=20,   StartY=0,   FinishX=0, FinishY=0)
16. }

17. -->
18. </style></head>
19. <body> <p>
20. <img   src="C:\\dog.jpg"   width=150   height=100   style="filter:alpha(Opacity=100, FinishOpacity=0,Style=2, StartX=30, StartY=50,FinishX=0, FinishY=0)" ALT="Alpha Image!">
21. <span> Alpha Mode</span> </p>
22. </body>
23. </HTML>

Blur effect

To create an image with a little blur, you need to use the CSS blur effect. The *add* means true or false. If added to blur it is *true,* otherwise is is false. The strength is **5px** by default unless you change it to a higher strength value.

<img src="dog.jpg" width="150" height="100"
style="Filter: Blur(Add = 0, Direction = 225, Strength = 8)">
span{
display:inline-block;
width:250; height:30;font-size:30px;
font-family:arial;color:# 000000;
font-weight:bold;Filter: Blur(Add = 1,   Direction = 225, Strength = 15)}

FlipH & FlipV

The flip effect can flip text horizontally, flipH, or vertically, flipV.

```
<img src="dog.jpg" width="150" height="100"
style="filter:fliph">
Span{ filter:fliph}
```

```
filter:flipv
<img src="dog.jpg" width="120" height="90"
style="filter:flipv">
```

Wave effect

Freq= frequency of wave
Strength = density
Light= strength of light on the wave motion (0-100)
Phase=sine wave degree (0-100)

Wave effect

You can see the effect of the wave with this simple example.

```
<img src="dog.jpg" width="120" height="90"
style="filter:Wave(Add=0, Freq=1, lightStrength=25,
Phase=90, Strength=10)">
```

More effects

There are more effects you can try. Look at all the rest.

• filter:xray
• filter:mask(color=#cccccc)
• filter:invert
• filter:gray
• filter:glow(color=#000000, strength=5)
• filter:dropshadow(color=#cccccc, offx=5, offy=9)

offx=number of drop shadow along X
offy=number of drop shadow along Y

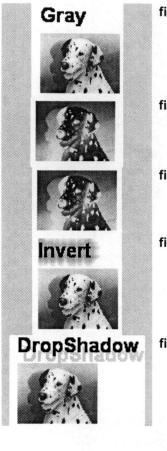

filter:gray

filter:xray

filter:invert

filter:glow(color=#00ff00, strength=10)

filter:dropshadow(color=#cccccc, offx=5, offy=9)

Laboratory exercises

1- Implement all of these CSS features
   1. Create a layout that satisfies all of the following conditions:
   2. Create a link "load Image".
   3. There must not be a bar under the link.
   4. When the mouse is placed on the link, the color becomes red, font becomes 16pt and bars display on the top and bottom.
   5. When user clicks, an image (any image) will display on the screen. The image must Flip Vertically.
   6. The name of your image must be in shadow format with different colors.

2-Create an external file in CSS that only contains a designed header. Call it *header.css*. Create a webpage that has a link from page2 to page3. When you click on any page, the same header should show. On page1 (the main page), create an overflow box with a scroll that will output a message.

3-Create a webpage. When your webpage has loaded, you should see an image (it could be any image, such as a cat). When the user clicks on the image once, it should Flip Horizontally. The second time, the image should Flip Vertically. By the third click, it should become blurry, and by the fourth click, the image should be wavy.

Chapter 13

CSS Layout and Menus

Introduction

In addition to image manipulation, CSS has many advanced features that allow us to create very interesting designs. With mouse-over, or *hover*, you can invoke the border of an object to changed as the mouse touches the object. The opacity plays an important role. Automatic image enlargement is also done by CSS. This chapter will also demonstrate transparency and the process of creating a box on the top of background. The most important part of this chapter is the implementation of the menu. We will try to show different menus both horizontally and vertically.

Effect of Mouse on button

One of the interesting features of CSS is its ability to change the behavior of the button when the button is linked to a webpage. The **hover** keyword is used in order to perform this feature.

Border effect

Hover can have an effect on the border or the position of a button. First, you must define your style in CSS and then apply it on the html code.

```
.bordering img
{
border: 2px solid red;
}
 .bordering:hover img
 {
 border: 3px solid blue;
 }
```

The **.bordering img** defines the solid static border, as the webpage is loaded. It will be displayed with a red colored border. The second part (in the shaded area), **.bordering:hover img**, is displayed when the user places a mouse on the link, and will change automatically according to the declared CSS style (the border becomes blue and thicker).

Example: 13.1
1. <!DOCTYPE HTML PUBLIC "-//W3C//DTD HTML 4.01//EN"
2. "http://www.w3.org/TR/html4/Strict.dtd">
3. <head>
4. <meta http-equiv="Content-Type" content="text/html; charset=iso-8859-1">
5. <title>Image Border Effect</title>
6. <style type="text/css" media="screen">
7. <!--
8. .bordering img{
9. border: 2px solid red; }
10..bordering:hover img {
11.border: 3px solid blue; }
12.-->

If you place a mouse on top of the image, you will see the color of the border automatically change to solid blue.

13.</style></head>
14.<body> <p>
15.<a href="http://www.shanbedi.com"
16.class="bordering"><img   src="c:\\button2.jpg"   width="80"   Alt="CSS   Border Effect"></a>
17.</p> </body>
18.</HTML>

More button effects

You may want to change the position of a button when the user puts the mouse on the top of the link, or you may be interested in making the button disappear during mouse activities.

When the mouse touches the link, the position of the button will change to 100px from the left, and the size of the button will become 100px in width.	.bordering img{
	border: 2px solid red;}
	.bordering:hover img{
	border: 3px solid blue;
	position: relative;
	left:100px; width:100px; }

As the mouse touches the button, it will disappear from the page.	.bordering img{
	border: 2px solid red;}
	.bordering:hover img{
	border: 3px solid blue; **display:none}**

Image link opacity

The opacity of an image significantly changes how a user sees that image. We can manipulate alpha-opacity in order to change the transparency of an image. The opacity of an image will change when the user places the mouse on top of it. The **onmouseover** keyword is used when the mouse is placed on the image. The **onmouseout** keyword is used when the mouse is out of the image territory.

Example: 13.2

```
1. <!DOCTYPE HTML PUBLIC "-//W3C//DTD HTML 4.01//EN"
2. "http://www.w3.org/TR/html4/Strict.dtd">
3. <head>
4. <meta http-equiv="Content-Type" content="text/html; charset=iso-8859-1">
5. <title>Transparency</title>
6. <style type="text/css" media="screen">
7. <!--
8. img {
9. filter : alpha(opacity=50); /* for IE browser*/
10.-moz-opacity: 0.5; /* For Mozilla */
11.}
12.-->
13.</style> </head> <body>
14.<h4>Image Opacity</h4> <p>
15.<a      href="http://www.shanbedi.com">      <img
   src="C:\\flower.jpg" Alt= "Image with Opacity!"
   width="100" height="80"
16.onmouseover="filters.alpha.opacity=100"
17.onmouseout="filters.alpha.opacity=30"> </a>
18.</p>
19.</body></html>
```

If you experience any problems with Mozilla then you may use this line:
onmouseout="this.style.MozOpacity=0.5; this.filters.alpha.opacity=50"
The value for **Mozilla** is 0 to 1, while for **IE** it is 0 to 100.
What happens if you change the opacity from (**30** to **0**) on line 17?
When *mouseover* the object it will be visible with full Opacity and when the *mouseout* the object it will be vanished from the screen.

Automatic image resizing

Image enlargement is one of the most interesting parts of CSS. Here we do not design anything related to the position of the image. You will see that when the page is first loaded, the image is 100px. Through using mouse-over, the image becomes 200px in width and after mouse-out, it returns to 70px in width.

Example: 13.3
1. <!DOCTYPE HTML PUBLIC "-//W3C//DTD HTML 4.01//EN"
2. "http://www.w3.org/TR/html4/Strict.dtd">
3. <head>
4. <meta http-equiv="Content-Type" content="text/html; charset=iso-8859-1">
5. <title>Automatic Enlargement</title>
6. <style type="text/css" media="screen">
7. </style>
8. </head>
9. <body>
10. <p>
11. <img src="C:\\donkey.jpg"style= "width:100px;"
12. onmouseover="this.style.width= '200px' "
13. onmouseout="this.style.width=' 70px' " >
14. </p>
15. </body>
16. </html>

A clash of old and modern within a society

Touch image by your mouse to expand

This is a *simple automatic image* enlargement. We use **onmouseover** for when the mouse is placed on top of the image and **onmouseout** when the mouse moves out of the image area. As the image is touched by mouse, the *width* size becomes 200px. The image returns to the normal size when the mouse leaves the image area.

Positioning enlargement

In the above example, the image enlargement has not been properly positioned. We have to design a CSS style and then apply it to the body of the program. Look at this example which outputs the same as the above example.

Example: 13.4
```
1.  <!DOCTYPE HTML PUBLIC "-//W3C//DTD HTML 4.01//EN"
2.  "http://www.w3.org/TR/html4/Strict.dtd">
3.  <head>
4.  <meta http-equiv="Content-Type" content="text/html; charset=iso-8859-1">
5.  <title>Positioning Enlargement</title>
6.  <style type="text/css" media="screen">
7.  <!--
8.  .Pic span{
9.  position: absolute;   background-color: #FFCC00;
10. padding: 2px; left:150;  top:30;   visibility: hidden; }
11. .Pic:hover span{   visibility: visible; }
12. -->
13. </style>   </head>   <body>   <p>
14. <a class="Pic" href="http://www.shanbedi.com">
15. <img src="C:\\donkey.jpg" Alt="positioning an image!" width="80px" height="50px" >
16. <span><img   src="C:\\donkey.jpg"   Alt="positioning   an   image!"   width="400"   >
    </span></a>   </p>
17. </body>
18. </html>
```

You see the background color that the image will be placed on. **Padding: 2px** indicates the size of padding around the image. The **position: absolute**; means that the top and left values are defined for enlargement. We define the enlargement size as 400 in width.

CSS layers

Layers are boxes or texts that can be placed one over another. In fact, color plays a really important role in layer building. Netscape may act differently regarding the layer layout. To create a layer, simply define the position (whether absolute or relative) and assign some values to the top and left of the layer. The **z-index** identifies which layer can be on the top. The layer with the bigger z-index number will be on the top.   There is no specific purpose for using layers, so every designer uses layers differently and for different reasons.

Example: 13.5
```
1.  <!DOCTYPE HTML PUBLIC "-//W3C//DTD HTML 4.01//EN"
2.  "http://www.w3.org/TR/html4/Strict.dtd">
3.  <head>
4.  <meta http-equiv="Content-Type" content="text/html; charset=iso-8859-1">
5.  <title>CSS Layers</title>
6.  <style type="text/css" media="screen">
7.  <!--
8.  h2 {
9.  position: relative;
10. top: 25px; left: 70px; z-index: 2;
11. background-color: #4169e1;
12. color: red; width:140px; height:120px;
13. overflow: hidden
14. }
15. div {
16. position: relative;
17. top:-50px; left:50; z-index: 1;
18. background-color: #bdb76b;
19. width:200px; height:120px; overflow: scroll
20. }
21. -->
22. </style> </head>
23. <body>
24. <h2 >
25. Layer #1 is positioned on the top!
26. </h2>
27. <div>
28. The layer number 2:
```

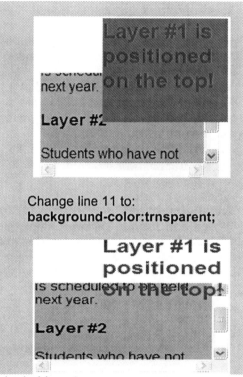

Change line 11 to:
background-color:trnsparent;

```
29. The final exam for winter term is scheduled to be held next year.
30. <h3> Layer #2 </h3> Students who have not learned this course properly may still
    delay the final examination!
31. </div> </body>
32. </html>
```

Transparency

Box transparency is a way to design the website. Sometimes you may want to create a popup menu that displays transparently. If you want to show some content and, at the same time have the page background be visible, then the box transparency is the best. Transparency is easy in CSS: you just set the **opacity** to the desired values. Once again, for **IE** the range is (0-100) and for **Mozilla** is (0-10).

Example: 13.6

```
1.  <!DOCTYPE HTML PUBLIC "-//W3C//DTD HTML 4.01//EN"
2.  "http://www.w3.org/TR/html4/Strict.dtd">
3.  <head>
4.  <meta http-equiv="Content-Type" content="text/html; charset=iso-8859-1">
5.  <title>Transparent Layers</title>
6.  <style type="text/css" media="screen">
7.  <!--
8.  div.back {
9.  width: 400px;   height: 250px; border: 1px groove;
10. background: url(c:\\deer.jpg) repeat; }
11. span.box {
12. display:inline-block; /* needed for IE*/
13. width: 300px;  height: 200px;  margin: 10px 30px;
14. background-color: #f8f8ff;  border: 2px solid red;
15. -moz-opacity:0.5; /*For Mozilla*/
16. filter:alpha(opacity=50); /*For IE*/
17. font-weight: bold;font-size:18px;
18. color: #000000;  }
19. -->
20. </style>  </HEAD>  <body>  <h2>Transparency</h2>
21. <p> The transparent box allows you
22. </p> <div class="back"> <span class="box">
23. to message out an important thing
24. related to your website while you still
25. see the background of the page.
26. </span> </div> </body>
27. </html>
```

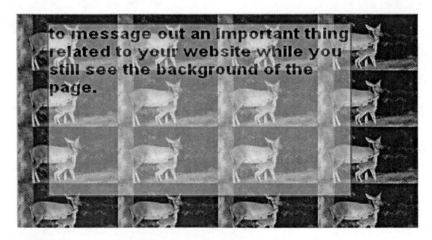

The box is surrounded by a red 2px border and is, therefore, fairly visible.

Menu

In modern layout design many webmasters use a menu, whether horizontal or vertical. The horizontal menus line up on a linear array which is clickable and linked to the related pages. The vertical menus are usually placed on the left or right in the navigating bar of the webpage. Menus sometimes contain submenus. There are several ways to create a menu. Some menus are loaded as image files.

Menus in HTML are usually done by using a table. In CSS you may AVOID using tables. In spite their sophistication the table also has some major problems.

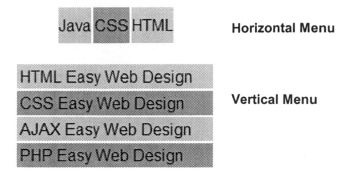

Horizontal Menu

Vertical Menu

Simple menu

CSS has the ability to generate different menus. There are two types of simple menus: a horizontal menu which is placed on the head of the page and a vertical menu which is usually placed on the right or left side of the page. The color of the menu plays a significant role.

Horizontal menu

The horizontal menu is more clear and visible simply because it placed on the top of the page. It is preferable when the size of the menu caption is precise.

Example: 13.7

```
1.  <!DOCTYPE HTML PUBLIC "-//W3C//DTD HTML 4.01//EN"
2.  "http://www.w3.org/TR/html4/Strict.dtd">
3.  <head>
4.  <meta http-equiv="Content-Type" content="text/html; charset=iso-8859-1">
5.  <title>Horizontal Menu</title>
6.  <style type="text/css" media="screen">
7.  <!--
8.  td.tb1 {
9.  background: #FFCC00;
10. font-size:16px;    font-weight: bold;
11. }
12. td.tb2 {
```

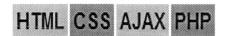

```
13.background: #999999;
14.font-size:16px; font-weight: bold;
15.}
16.-->
17.</style></head>      <body>
18.<table  cellpadding="3" >
19.<tr><td class="tb1"> HTML </td>
20.<td class="tb2">CSS </td>
21.<td class="tb1">AJAX </td>
22.<td class="tb2">
23.PHP </td> </tr> </table> </body>
24.</html>
```

The caption of each cell is precise. The background color is different, so it will be more visible.

You will see that instead of "HTML Easy Design", we just use a short text caption like "HTML"

Vertical menu

The vertical menu is preferable when the length of the text is a little longer than just one word. For example, instead of just typing HTML, you may want to use the full name like *HTML Easy Web Design*.

Example: 13.8

```
1.  <!DOCTYPE HTML PUBLIC "-//W3C//DTD HTML 4.01//EN"
2.  "http://www.w3.org/TR/html4/Strict.dtd">
3.  <head>
4.  <meta http-equiv="Content-Type" content="text/html; charset=iso-8859-1">
5.  <title>Vertical Menu</title>
6.  <style type="text/css" media="screen">
7.  <!--
8.  tr.tb1 {
9.  background: #FFCC00;  font-size:16px; font-weight: bold;
10.}
11.tr.tb2 {
12.background: #999999;  font-size:16px; font-weight: bold;
13.}
14.-->
15.</style> </head> <body>
16.<table width="200" cellpadding="3" >
17.<tr class="tb1"><td>
18.HTML Easy Web Design</td>
19.</tr> <tr class="tb2"><td>
20.CSS Easy Web Design</td>
21.</tr> <tr class="tb1"><td>
22.AJAX Easy Web Design</td>
23.<tr class="tb2"><td>
24.PHP Easy Web Design</td>
25.</tr> </table> </body>
26.</html>
```

| HTML Easy Web Design |
| CSS Easy Web Design |
| AJAX Easy Web Design |
| PHP Easy Web Design |

The cellpadding="3" creates spaces between each menu bar.

Automatic highlighting background

Onmouseover =" this.className and **onmouseout** = "this.className = 'tb1'" changes the background according to the pre-set background. We can use hover for this is simple background manipulation because it provides better functionalities.

Example: 13.9
1.   <!DOCTYPE HTML PUBLIC "-//W3C//DTD HTML 4.01//EN"
2.   "http://www.w3.org/TR/html4/Strict.dtd">
3.   <head>
4.   <meta http-equiv="Content-Type" content="text/html; charset=iso-8859-1">
5.   <title>Automatic Highlighting</title>
6.   <style type="text/css" media="screen">
7.   <!--
8.   td.tb1 {
9.   background: #FFCC00; font-size:16px; font-weight: bold;
10. }
11. td.tb2 {
12. background: #999999; font-size:16px; font-weight: bold;
13. }
14. -->
15. </style> </head> <body>
16. <table cellpadding="6" >
17. <tr><td class="tb1" onmouseover="this.className='tb2' "
18. onmouseout="this.className ='tb1'">HTML </td>
19. <td class="tb1" onmouseover="this.className='tb2'"
20. onmouseout="this.className='tb1'">CSS </td></tr>
21. </table> </body>
22. </html>

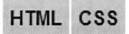

Just put your mouse on the above button and see how the background of button is changed.

Vertical background change

The <UL> and <LI> styles provide better menus compared to what a table can do. Here you do not need to create a table. The reality is that all menus are linked to some websites or files, so we can change the behavior of the hover, link, active and visited, etc.

Example: 13.10
1.   <!DOCTYPE HTML PUBLIC "-//W3C//DTD HTML 4.01//EN"
2.   "http://www.w3.org/TR/html4/Strict.dtd">
3.   <head>
4.   <meta http-equiv="Content-Type" content="text/html; charset=iso-8859-1">
5.   <title>Automatic Highlighting</title>

```
6.   <style type="text/css" media="screen">
7.   <!--
8.   td.tb1 {
9.   background: #FFCC00;
10.  font-size:16px; font-weight: bold;
11.  height: 25px; width:200px;
12.  border: ridge yellow;
13.  }
14.  td.tb2 {
15.  background: #999999;
16.  font-size:16px; font-weight: bold;
17.  height: 30px;width:250px;
18.  border: ridge yellow; text-align:center;
19.  }
20.  -->
21.  </style> </head> <body>
22.  <table  cellpadding="6" >
23.  <tr><td class="tb1" onmouseover="this.className='tb2' "
24.  onmouseout="this.className ='tb1'">HTML and CSS </td></tr>
25.  <tr> <td class="tb1" onmouseover="this.className='tb2'"
26.  onmouseout="this.className='tb1'">PHP and MySQL </td></tr>
27.  <tr> <td class="tb1" onmouseover="this.className='tb2'"
28.  onmouseout="this.className='tb1'"><a href="http://www.dreamweaver.com"
     style="text-decoration:none" >Ajax </a></td></tr>
29.  <tr> <td class="tb1" onmouseover="this.className='tb2'"
30.  onmouseout="this.className='tb1'"><a href="http://www.JavaScript.com"
     style="text-decoration:none" >JavaScript</a></td></tr>
31.  </table> </body>
32.  </html>
```

When you put the mouse on the menu link, the background color will automatically change and also watch another two changes, the text caption moves to the center and button size will enlarge.

You can call the menu by <div id="menu"> and use <UL> in order to output the bullets beside the menu. Here we made the border a little thicker in order to be more visible. You can use a tiny border which also looks nice!

```
<div id="menu">
<ul>
<li><a href="#" >JAVA </a></li>
<li><a href="#" >JSP   </a></li>
</ul>
<div>
```

- HTML Easy Web Design
- CSS Easy Web Design
- AJAX Easy Web Design
- PHP Easy Web Design
- JAVA Advanced Web Design
- JSP Advanced Web Design

You may want to have an "angle quotation mark (right)" right in front of the menu caption, so you can use "**»**". We use "** **" in order to have some space after the" **»** ".

» HTML Easy Web Design

» CSS Easy Web Design

» JavaScript Easy Web Design

» AJAX Easy Web Design

» PHP Easy Web Design

» JAVA Advanced Web Design

» JSP Advanced Web Design

```
<ul id="menu">
<li><a href="#"> &raquo;   HTML
Easy Web Design</a></li>
<li><a    href="#"   >&raquo; CSS
Easy Web Design</a></li>
</ul>
```

Menu buttons
Attaching images in CSS is mostly done by using a background or a background-image such as **background-image: url(menu1.gif);**, where the menu1.gif is the file name. In order to see a different menu or a different color, you must use hover which will invoke another image to load, as with **background-image:url(menu2.gif);**. In this instance, the two files, **menu1.gif** and **menu2.gif**, are the exactly same; they differ only in color.
In the above example, if you shrink the margin by using negative numbers then you will see this nice looking menu: *Margin: -18px;*

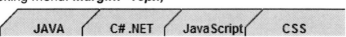

Example: 13.11

```
1. <!DOCTYPE HTML PUBLIC "-//W3C//DTD HTML 4.01//EN"
2. "http://www.w3.org/TR/html4/Strict.dtd">
3. <head>
4. <meta http-equiv="Content-Type" content="text/html; charset=iso-8859-1">
5. <title>buttons background</title>
6. <style type="text/css" media="screen">
7. <!--
8. .menu a{
9. text-decoration: none;  font: bold 12px Arial; color: black;
10.width: 100px; height: 20px; float:left; margin-right: 0px;
11.background-image:url(C:\\menu2.gif);
12.background-repeat: no-repeat;
13.padding-top: 12px; text-align:center; }
14..menu a:hover{
15.background-image:url(C:\\menu1.gif); }
16.-->
17.</style> </head>
18.<body>
19.<div class="menu">
20.<a href="#">JAVA </a> <a href="#">C# .NET </a>
21.<a href="#">JavaScript </a> <a href="#">CSS</a>
22.<br><br>
23.</div><h4>Welcome to background Images</h4>
24.</body>
25.</html>
```

Vertical menu button

In the previous example we created a horizontal button menu by loading an image. Now we want to do the same thing, but this time with vertical menus in which images are displayed vertically. First the **float :left** has to be removed because it isused for horizontal menus. In vertical menus, we use the <UL> which is the best option to create a vertical menu. Wherever there is a problem with the **<LI>** tag, it simply outputs a bullet in front of each image. You need to use **UL { list-style:none; }** in order to remove this bullet.

Example: 13.12

```
1. <!DOCTYPE HTML PUBLIC "-//W3C//DTD HTML 4.01//EN"
2. "http://www.w3.org/TR/html4/Strict.dtd">
3. <head>
4. <meta http-equiv="Content-Type" content="text/html; charset=iso-8859-1">
5. <title>Buttons background</title>
6. <style type="text/css" media="screen">
7. <!--
```

```
8.  .menu a{
9.  display:inline-block;
10.text-decoration: none;
11.font: bold 12px Arial;  color: black;
12.width: 150px; height: 20px;  margin-right: 5px;
13.background-image:url(C:\\menu1.gif);
14.background-repeat: no-repeat;
15.padding-top: 10px; text-align:center; }
16..menu a:hover {
17.background-image:url(C:\\menu2.gif);
18.}
19.UI { list-style:none; }
20.-->
21.</style></head>        <body>
22.<ul class="menu">
23.<li><a href="#">JAVA Programming</a></li>
24.<li><a href="#">C# .NET </a></li>
25.<li><a href="#">JavaScript </a></li>
26.<li><a href="#">CSS Web Design</a></li>
27.</UL>
28.</body>
29.</html>
```

You can use any other image.

The image will change when the user places the mouse on it. First, the menu1.gif will appear and then the menu2.gif file will display because of **hover**.

If you remove line 8 "**background-image:url(menu1.gif);** ", the image will load and you will only see the text. The image menu2.gif is activated by placing a mouse on the text.

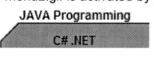

JavaScript

CSS Web Design

Laboratory exercises

1-Create a webpage which upon loading, an image will show on the screen. Use an image of a goat, sized 100 X 100. When the user puts the mouse on the image, it should automatically enlarge to 200 X 200 and, instead of being a goat, it should change into a camel.

2- Design a simple page with a nice background. On the top of the page, use a red layer to write, "Welcome to my site". Make another blue layer on the top half of the layer in order to write "See Yahoo page". Load an image inside the webpage. When you put your mouse on the image, its opacity will change automatically. Use any density for the opacity.

3- Design a nice layout containing both horizontal and vertical menus. On the horizontal menu use some button images with these captions: Home, Tutorials, Ajax and Java, which will change color upon using mouse-over. Place your vertical menu on the left (20%). The menus are set vertically and, by putting a mouse on any of the menus, they should become shadowy or display a button.

Part III
XHTML Web Design

Chapter 14

XHTML

Introduction

HTML is intended to display pages. However today, with the presence of different browser technology, poorly formatted HTML may create problem. New technology, such as handheld devices, requires better scripting technology. The XHTML is a well-formed version of HTML; therefore it describes data and works under browsers that are designed to handle XML (the future of Internet technology). As HTML is designed to display data, XML is designed to describe data. In this chapter we will demonstrate many examples that make XHTML easy to understand.

What is XHTML

XHTML stands for e**X**tensible **H**yper **T**ext **M**arkup **L**anguage. In fact, it is a bridge between HTML and XML. XHTML allows us to create a stricter standard for making web pages and removes the problems found with browsers in a significant way. It works with different devices without any changes. The XHTML code is almost the same as HTML, but with some small differences. XHTML helps you to create fully formatted code on your web page. XHTML is aimed to replace HTML, providing us with better web pages.

HTML vs. XHTML

◆ Unlike HTML, the XHTML must be properly nested. Look at this statement:

`<b><i> This is OK for HTML but NOT OK for XHTML</b></i>`

You see the `<b>` is closed before the `<i>`, which is not correct on the nested format.

◆ XHTML tags must always be in lowercase.

`<p> every thing will be in lowercase</p>`

◆ XHTML tags must be closed. In HTML you can leave some tags unclosed.

`<html><b> OK for HTML not OK for XHTML</b>`

You see the `<html>` tag is not closed.

◆ In HTML, you can use a shortcut, *attribute-name-value,* or omit the attribute-name. In XHTML, attributes must always be used within quotation marks and quotations are always necessary (as either single or double quotes).

You can use shortcut attributes in HTML such as,

`<option          name=China          selected>China</option          >`

in XHTML you need to use an attribute like,

`<option name="China" selected="selected">China</option>`

◆ XHTML code must have one root element. In this case, the root element may well be the `<html>` tag. Every other element must be nested correctly.
◆ Errors are fatal in XHTML, but they are they are forgivable in HTML.
◆ XHTML is case sensitive while HTML is not.

DTD for XHTML

The **<!DOCTYPE>** tag is used to declare the Document Type Definition (DTD) for an XHTML document. It has to be declared at the beginning of the page (on the top, first line of the code). In fact, `<!DOCTYPE>` tells browsers what document specification must be used (HTML or XHTML).

There are three types of **DTDs** used in XHTML: **Strict**, **Transitional**, and **Frameset**, we use the same way as we used for HTML.

Strict is declared when you use **C**ascading **S**tyle **S**heets (CSS) to enhance the style of your HTML document. The strict does not allow any deprecated tags. This is the syntax:

`<!DOCTYPE html PUBLIC "-//W3C//DTD XHTML 1.0 Strict//EN" "http://www.w3.org/TR/xhtml1/DTD/xhtml1-strict.dtd">`

Transitional: Use this DTD type when you use HTML rather than CSS. If you have a wide variety of viewers, you can use the transitional type. Usually we use transitional (loose) when we have an HTML file with some deprecated elements. The syntax is:

```
<!DOCTYPE html PUBLIC "-//W3C//DTD XHTML 1.0 Transitional//EN"
"http://www.w3.org/TR/xhtml1/DTD/xhtml1-transitional.dtd">
```

Frameset: This type is used when you have several frames in your pages and have some deprecated tags. It can be used with or without CSS. The syntax is:

```
<!DOCTYPE html PUBLIC "-//W3C//DTD XHTML 1.0 Frameset//EN"
"http://www.w3.org/TR/xhtml1/DTD/xhtml1-frameset.dtd " >
```

▶ **Note:** Unlike XHTML tags, which must be closed on a appropriate places, the **<!DOCTYPE>** does not need to be closed. Use of exclamation sign (!) is required.

The W3C recommends using XML DOCTYPE on the first line as an option (this is NOT necessary).

<?xml version="1.0" encoding="iso-8859-1"?>

XHTML general format

XHTML document contains these three parts:
◆ DOCTYPE
◆ head
◆ body

Here, look at an example of a simple document in XHTML.

XHTML Source Document	XML Diagram shows open and closed tags (Well-Formed)

`<?xml version="1.0" encoding="UTF-8"?>`
`<!DOCTYPE html PUBLIC "-//W3C//DTD XHTML 1.0 strict//EN"`
` "http://www.w3.org/TR/xhtml1/DTD/xhtml1-Strict.dtd">`
` <html xmlns="http://www.w3.org/1999/xhtml" lang="en" xml:lang="en">`
`<head>`
`<title>Simple Document </title>`
`</head>`
`<body>`
`<p>Document body! </p>`
`</body>`
`</html>`
	html
	 head
	  title Simple Document title
	 head
	 body
	  p Document body! p
	 body
	html

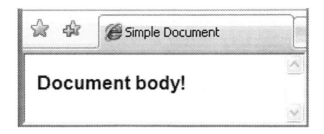

The DOCTYPE may also be similar to this:

> *<?xml version="1.0" encoding="UTF-8"?>*
> *<!DOCTYPE html*
> *PUBLIC "-//W3C//DTD XHTML 1.0 Strict//EN"*
> *"DTD/xhtml1-strict.dtd">*
> *<html xmlns="http://www.w3.org/1999/xhtml" lang="EN">*

XHTML tags

In fact, many XHTML tags are the same as HTML tags. You already know that some HTML tags have been deprecated, so you may use the style sheet (CSS) instead. When you write XHTML documents you must respect the nested tags.

<b><i> XHTML<b><i>   This tag is wrong
<b><i> XHTML<i><b>   This tag is correct

Some tags, like <hr> and <br>, which are known as empty tags and do not need to be closed in the HTML, have to be closed by a *slash-forward* in XHTML. Look at some empty tags that need to be close by a "/" in XHTML.

** **	**<link />**
<hr />	**<base />**
<img />	**<param />**
<input />	**<mata />**

▶ **Note:** Make sure you have extra space between the element and the slash-forward, like **
** and NOT **
. This is the general form for <hr /> tag: **<hr size="n" />

Example: 14.1
1. **<?xml version="1.0" encoding="UTF-8"?>**
2. **<!DOCTYPE html PUBLIC "-//W3C//DTD XHTML 1.0 Transitional//EN"**
3. **"http://www.w3.org/TR/xhtml1/DTD/xhtml1-Transitional.dtd">**
4. **<html xmlns="http://www.w3.org/1999/xhtml" lang="en" xml:lang="en">**
5. <head>
6. <title> XHTML Horizontal Line </title>
7. </head>
8. <body bgcolor="silver">

```
<hr align="center" width="400" size="10" />
<hr align="center" width="350" size="9" />
<hr align="center" width="300" size="8" />
<hr align="center" width="250" size="7" />
<hr align="center" width="200" size="6" />
<hr align="center" width="150" size="5" />
<hr align="center" width="100" size="4" />
<hr align="center" width="50" size="3" />
<br />
</body>
</html>
```

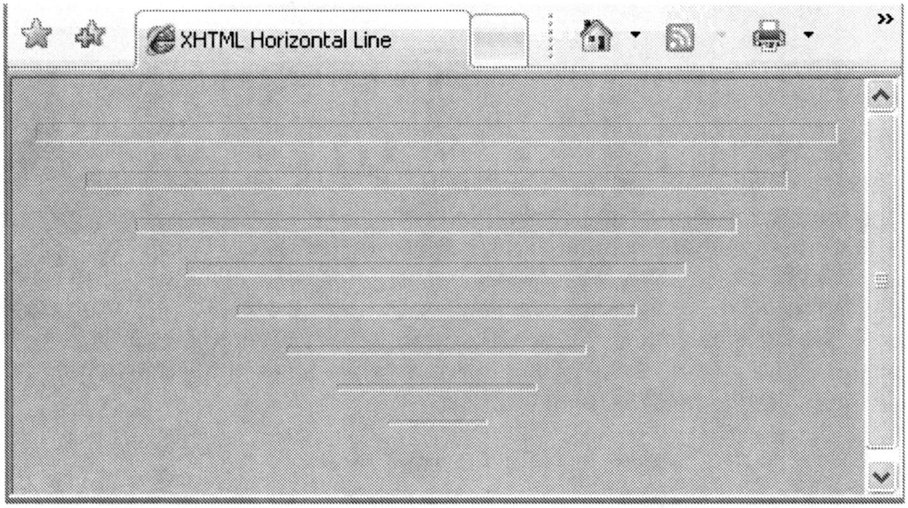

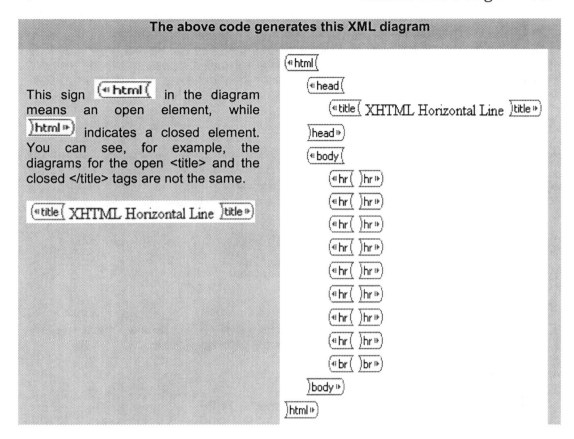

The above code generates this XML diagram

This sign ❨◂html❨ in the diagram means an open element, while ❩html▸❩ indicates a closed element. You can see, for example, the diagrams for the open <title> and the closed </title> tags are not the same.

❨◂title❨ XHTML Horizontal Line ❩title▸❩

Attribute rules

In XHTML, attributes contain some rules that have to be respected.

• **Lowercase name:**
<table width="50%"> the width must be in lowercase NOT WIDTH.

• **Quotation:**
The values must be enclosed in a quotation:
<table width="50%"> the 50% is in quotation

• **Full attribute**
The attribute must not be minimized like in HTML.
<option selected="selected" />
You can see that instead of <option selected> in HTML format, we use *<option selected=**"selected"** />*

• **Id and name**
Use both id and name attribute together to be compatible with older browsers.

XHTML Validation

It is very helpful to validate your code with one of the free *validators* that provide service for the Internet. Some of links to these validators are stated below. When you visit the related validators you can call your file from your local directory, as well as from your website.

http://www.htmlvalidator.com/
http://validator.w3.org/
http://onlinewebcheck.com/

All codes in this book have been validated for clarity
You can use the related *logo* from W3C, after the code has validated.

Colors and fonts

Font and color follow HTML rules with the exception that XHTML is case sensitive (every thing must be in lower case) and the attributes must be in quotations.
<Font color= "#FFCC50"> this is not correct
<font color="#ffcc33"> this is correct in XHTML.

Example: 14.2
1. <?xml version="1.0" encoding="UTF-8"?>
2. <!DOCTYPE html PUBLIC "-//W3C//DTD XHTML 1.0 Transitional//EN"
3. "http:// www.w3.org/TR /xhtml1/DTD/ xhtml1-Transitional.dtd">
4. <html xmlns="http://www.w3.org/1999/xhtml" lang="en" xml:lang="en">
5. <head>
6. <title>Color, Font, Background</title>
7. </head>
8. <body bgcolor="silver">
9. <font color="maroon" size="+4" face="Courier">
10. Silver Background
Maroon text</font>
11. </body>
12. </html>

Images

The <img /> tag is a self-closing tag which does need a closing tag </img>. The <img /> tag is designed to deal with graphics and images with different formats. Its attributes are **alt, align, border, height, width, hspace, vspace and title**.

We put all attributes on a line along with <img />
<img src="pic4.jpg" **align**="left" **width**= "180" **height**="80" **alt**="The **gorgeous blue flowers**" **border** ="5" />

Example: 14.3
1. <?xml version="1.0" encoding="UTF-8"?>
2. <!DOCTYPE html PUBLIC "-//W3C//DTD XHTML 1.0 Transitional//EN"
3. "http://www.w3.org/TR/xhtml1/DTD/xhtml1-Transitional.dtd">
4. <html xmlns="http://www.w3.org/1999/xhtml" lang="en" xml:lang="en">
5. <head>
6. <title>XHTML image</title>
7. </head>
8. <body>
9. <img src="pic4.jpg" align="left" width="180" height="80" alt="The gorgeous blue flowers" border="5" />
10. </body>
11. </html>

You can generate an image as the background.
<body background="pic4.jpg">
</body>

Tables

Tables are used for presenting and displaying data on screen. The data can be read from the database system and shown as a tabular format. In addition to **tr**, **td** and **th**, XHTML provides **tbody**, **tfoot** and **thead**.
Cellpadding and CellSpacing: The Cellpadding sets space between text and the wall of table.
<table border="2" cellpadding="5"> </table>

Cellspacing sets space between two cells:
<table border="2" cellspacing="5"> </table>

The table border can be in color:
<table border="5" **bordercolor**= "red"> </table> However, since it is not supported anymore, use CSS style.

You can attach an image as the background of a table:
<table border="2" **background**="file.gif"> </table> However, since this is not supported anymore, use CSS style.

You can use **valign** and **haling** for vertical and horizontal align.
The **nowrap** attribute is supported in XHTML.
You can use **void** (without border), **vsides**(with vertical border only), **hsides**(Horizontal border only), **rhs**(right border only) or **lhs**(left sides).

Example: 14.4

1. <?xml version="1.0" encoding="UTF-8"?>
2. <!DOCTYPE html PUBLIC "-//W3C//DTD XHTML 1.0 Transitional//EN"
3. "http://www.w3.org/TR/xhtml1/DTD/xhtml1-Transitional.dtd">
4. <html xmlns="http://www.w3.org/1999/xhtml" lang="en" xml:lang="en">
5. <head>
6. <title>Table in XHTML</title>
7. </head> <body>
8. <table border="3" frame="vsides">
9. <caption>1- Vertical Sides</caption>
10. <tr> <td> (Row-0,Col-0)</td><td>(Row-0,Col-1)</td>
11. </tr> <tr>
12. <td>(Row-1,Col-0)</td> <td>(Row-1,Col-1)</td>
13. </tr> </table>
14. <table border="3" frame="hsides">
15. <caption>2- Horizontal Sides</caption>
16. <tr> <td> (Row-0,Col-0)</td><td>(Row-0,Col-1)</td>
17. </tr> <tr>
18. <td>(Row-1,Col-0)</td> <td>(Row-1,Col-1)</td>
19. </tr> </table>
20. <table border="3" frame="rhs">
21. <caption>3- Right Sides</caption>
22. <tr> <td> (Row-0,Col-0)</td><td>(Row-0,Col-1)</td>
23. </tr> <tr> <td>(Row-1,Col-0)</td> <td>(Row-1,Col-1)</td>
24. </tr> </table>
25.
 <table frame="void">
26. <caption> 4- No Sides </caption>
27. <tr> <td> (Row-0,Col-0)</td><td>(Row-0,Col-1)</td>
28. </tr> <tr>
29. <td>(Row-1,Col-0)</td> <td>(Row-1,Col-1)</td>

30.</tr> </table> </body>
31.</html>

1- Vertical Sides

(Row-0,Col-0)	(Row-0,Col-1)
(Row-1,Col-0)	(Row-1,Col-1)

3- Right Sides

(Row-0,Col-0)	(Row-0,Col-1)
(Row-1,Col-0)	(Row-1,Col-1)

2- Horizontal Sides

(Row-0,Col-0)	(Row-0,Col-1)
(Row-1,Col-0)	(Row-1,Col-1)

4- No Sides

(Row-0,Col-0) (Row-0,Col-1)
(Row-1,Col-0) (Row-1,Col-1)

We can design a table with the power of CSS. CSS is all about design, whereas HTML is about contents and JavaScript is about behavior.

Example: 14.5

1. <?xml version="1.0" encoding="UTF-8"?>
2. <!DOCTYPE html PUBLIC "-//W3C//DTD XHTML 1.0 Transitional//EN"
3. "http://www.w3.org/TR/xhtml1/DTD/xhtml1-Transitional.dtd">
4. <html xmlns="http://www.w3.org/1999/xhtml" lang="en" xml:lang="en">
5. <head> <title>Table in XHTML</title>
6. <style type= "text/css" >
7. TABLE { border: outset 12pt;
8. border-collapse: separate;
9. border-spacing: 12pt; }
10. TD { border: inset 6pt; }
11. TD { color:blue; }
12. </style> </head> <body>
13. <table>
14. <caption> Designed Table </caption>
15. <tr> <td> (Row-0,Col-0) </td><td>(Row-0,Col-1)</td>
16. </tr> <tr>
17. <td>(Row-1,Col-0)</td> <td>(Row-1,Col-1) </td>
18. </tr>
19.   </table> </body> </html>

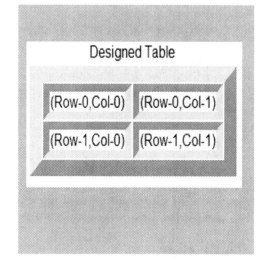

Forms

As we have already seen, a form is a way that allows us to enter data into designed boxes. The general format will be simple, such as **<form> ... </form>**. The form can have one or several input boxes: select, text area, text field, password field, checkbox, radio, submit and button.

Text field

The text field allows us to use an input box that is editable. You can enter data in the text field (name, postal code and ...).   The text field needs some captions, for which you can use the <label> tag. In fact, you may use the label tag on almost every form element except buttons. You will use *name* and *id* for each input box. You will use this more later.

Example: 14.6

1. *<?xml version="1.0" encoding="UTF-8"?>*
2. *<!DOCTYPE html PUBLIC "-//W3C//DTD XHTML 1.0 Strict//EN"*
3. *"http://www.w3.org/TR/xhtml1/DTD/xhtml1-Strict.dtd">*
4. *<html xmlns="http://www.w3.org/1999/xhtml" lang="en" xml:lang="en">*
5. <head>
6. <title>XHTML Password Fields</title>
7. </head>
8. <body>
9. **<form** action="" method="post">
10. <p>
11. <label for="txtEmail">Email:</label>
12. <input class="input" type="text" title="Enter your Email, max 20 characters"
13. maxlength="20" size="25" name="Email" id="txtEmail" value="Email box"/>
14.
15. <label for="txtpass"> Password: </label>
16. <input class="input" type= "password" title="Input password"
17. maxlength="8" size="25" name="password" id="txtpass" value="password box"/>
18. </p> **</form>**
19. </body> </html>

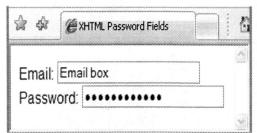

Maximum length of the text box is set to 20 characters and the password box is set to 8. Therefore, it is impossible to enter more than the limited size.

On line 9 you see **<form** action="" method="post">. At this point, do not worry about the "**action**" and the "**post**". These are set for the server side, and we are not dealing with the server side here. You will learn it in *PHP* and *MySQL* book.

Radio box

The Radio box is designed to operate two stated values, namely True or False. It creates an empty circle and permits users to check only one box among many.

Example: 14.7
1. <?xml version="1.0" encoding="UTF-8"?>
2. <!DOCTYPE html PUBLIC "-//W3C//DTD XHTML 1.0 Strict//EN"
3. "http://www.w3.org/TR/xhtml1/DTD/xhtml1-Strict.dtd">
4. <html xmlns="http://www.w3.org/1999/xhtml" lang="en" xml:lang="en">
5. <head>
6. <title>XHTML Radio</title>
7. </head>
8. <body>
9. <form action="" method="post">
10. <p> Do you agree?
11. <label for="radio1">Yes:</label>
12. <input class="input" type="radio" title="This is yes option!"
13. name="Agree" id="radios" value ="Yes"/>
14.
15. <label for="radios"> No:</label>
16. <input class="input" type="radio" title="this is no option!"
17. name="Agree" id="radio2" value="No"/>
18. </p>
19. </form> </body>
20. </html>

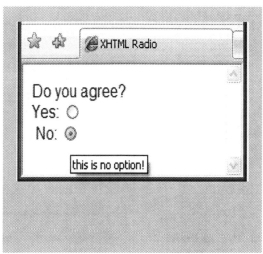

You have two options: Yes or No. If one is true then the rest automatically are false.

Checkbox
The checkbox syntax is similar to the radio box except that users can choose many options at the same time.

Example: 14.8
1. <?xml version="1.0" encoding="UTF-8"?>
2. <!DOCTYPE html PUBLIC "-//W3C//DTD XHTML 1.0 Strict//EN"
3. "http://www.w3.org/TR/xhtml1/DTD/xhtml1-Strict.dtd">
4. <html xmlns="http://www.w3.org/1999/xhtml" lang="en" xml:lang="en">
5. <head>
6. <title>XHTML Checkbox</title>
7. </head> <body>
8. **<form action="" method="post">**
9. <p> Choose one or many options :
10. <input class="input" type="checkbox" title="HTML option!"
11. name="check1" id="check1" value=""/>
12. <label for="check1">HTML</label>
13.
 <input class="input" type="checkbox" title="CSS option!"
14. name="check2" id="check2" value=""/>
15. <label for="check2"> CSS</label>

```
16. <br /> <input class="input" type="checkbox" title="Ajax option!"
17. name="check3" id="check3" value=""/>
18. <label for="check3">AJAX</label>
19. <br /> <input class="input" type="checkbox" title="PHP and MySQL option!"
20. name="check4" id="check4" value=""/>
21. <label for="check4">  PHP</label>
22. </p> </form> </body>
23. </html>
```

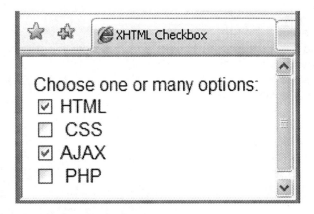

In the above example, we changed the arrangement of the checkboxes to line up on the left of their captions, like ☑ HTML instead of HTML ☑

Text Area

The keyword *textarea* is recognized by every browser. You must assign numbers to rows and columns like rows="5" cols="50". The vertical scroll bar in IE is automatically activated. It is designed to handle text.

Example: 14.9
```
1.  <?xml version="1.0" encoding="UTF-8"?>
2.  <!DOCTYPE html PUBLIC "-//W3C//DTD XHTML 1.0 Strict//EN"
3.  "http://www.w3.org/TR/xhtml1/DTD/xhtml1-Strict.dtd">
4.  <html xmlns="http://www.w3.org/1999/xhtml" lang="en" xml:lang="en">
5.  <head>
6.  <title>XHTML Text Area</title>
7.  </head> <body>
8.  <form action="" method="post">
9.  <p> <label for="Area1">Type you comments here!</label><br />
10. <textarea  rows="5" cols="30" title="This is a text area!"
11. name="Area1" id="Area1"></textarea>  </p>
12. </form> </body> </html>
```

Type you comments here!

```
On 1935 the Persia has been
changed to Iran. Western
countries still using Persia,
instead of Iran.
```

Combo box

Combo box is known as a drop-down list and is understood as "**select**" by browsers. It can handle many elements and save space in your webpage. The user can only select one option at a time. Syntax:

<select> <option> ... </option> </select>

Example: 14.10

1. `<?xml version="1.0" encoding="UTF-8"?>`
2. `<!DOCTYPE html PUBLIC "-//W3C// DTD XHTML 1.0 Strict//EN"`
3. `"http://www.w3.org/TR/xhtml1/DTD/xhtml1-Strict.dtd">`
4. `<html xmlns="http://www.w3.org/1999/ xhtml" lang="en" xml:lang="en">`
5. `<head>`
6. `<title>XHTML Combobox</title>`
7. `</head>`
8. `<body>`
9. `<form action="" method="post">`
10. `<p>`
11. `<label for="cmb">Choose an option!</label><br />`
12. `<select title="select an item form Combo-box!" name="cmb" id= "cmb">`
13. `<option value=""> Choose one!</option>`
14. `<option value="Green"> Green</option>`
15. `<option value="Red">  Red</option>`
16. `<option value="Yellow"> Yellow</option>`
17. `<option value="Maroon"> Maroon</option>`
18. `</select>`
19. `</p>`
20. `</form> </body>`
21. `</html>`

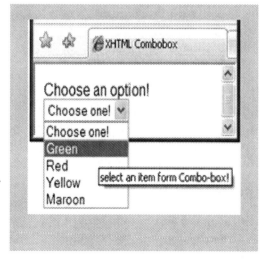

Grouping elements

So far we worked on different parts of the form. Now is the time to put them all together. The **fieldset** tag is used to group related form elements. It creates a caption using the **legend** tag.

Example: 14.11

1. `<?xml version="1.0" encoding="UTF-8"?>`
2. `<!DOCTYPE html PUBLIC "-//W3C//DTD XHTML 1.0 Strict//EN"`
    `"http://www.w3.org/TR/xhtml1/DTD/xhtml1-Strict.dtd">`
3. `<html xmlns="http://www.w3.org/1999/xhtml" lang="en" xml:lang="en">`
4. `<head>`
5. `<title> XHTML Fieldset </title>`
6. `</head>`
7. `<body>`
8. `<form action="" method="post">`
9. `<table style="width:30%"><tr><td>`
10. `<fieldset>`
11. `<legend>Please login:</legend>`
12. `<p>`
13. `<label for="user">User Name: </label> <br`
    `/> <input type="text" id="user" />`
14. `<br />`
15. `<label for="pass"> Password: </label> <br`
    `/> <input type="password" id="pass" />`
16. `</p> </fieldset>`
17. `</td> </tr> </table>`
18. `</form> </body>`
19. `</html>`

Grouping Combo-box

We use optgroup (option group) and fieldset along with legend. The OPTGROUP can create different groups within the same <select>. OPTGROUP must contain one or more OPTION elements to build the combo-box.

Example: 14.12

1. `<?xml version="1.0" encoding="UTF-8"?>`
2. `<!DOCTYPE html PUBLIC "-//W3C//DTD XHTML 1.0 Strict//EN"`
3. `"http://www.w3.org/TR/xhtml1/DTD/xhtml1-Strict.dtd">`
4. `<html xmlns="http://www.w3.org/1999/xhtml" lang="en" xml:lang="en">`
5. `<head>`
6. `<title>OPTGROUP</title>`
7. `</head>`
8. `<body> <table style="width:30%"><tr><td>`
9. `<fieldset>`
10. `<legend>Travel Agency</legend>`
11. `<form action="" method="post">`

```
12. <p>
13. <label for="cities">Choose your destination</label><br />
14. <select name="city" id="cities">
15. <optgroup label="West Europe">
16. <option value="1">UK</option>
17. <option value="2">France</option>
18. </optgroup>
19. <optgroup label="East Europe">
20. <option value="3">Poland</option>
21. <option value="4">Hungary</option>
22. </optgroup>
23. <optgroup label="North America">
24. <option value="5">Canada</option>
25. <option value="6">USA</option>
26. </optgroup>
27. <optgroup label="Middle East">
28. <option value="7">Iran(Persia)</option>
29. <option value="8">UAE</option>
30. </optgroup> </select>
31. </p> </form> </fieldset>
32. </td> </tr> </table> </body>
33. </html>
```

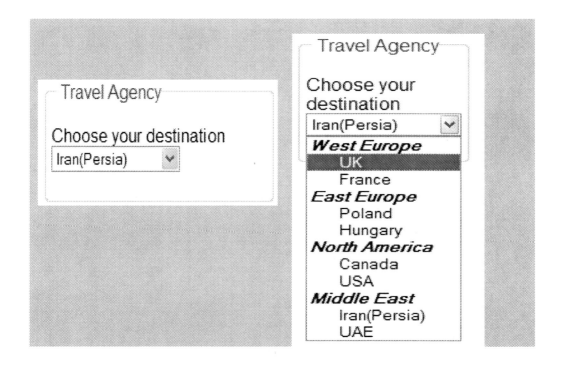

Now what?

After successfully completing this book, you will need to work on JavaScript. This is a dynamic and amazing script for creating websites (client-side). You will also need to study PHP and MySQL, which gives you full webpage building skills (both client and server sides). There are many tools that you can work with when you have sufficient knowledge of web programming.

Review questions

1- What does **XHTML** stand for?

2-In XHTML, if we do not properly nest tags, still code is still valid.	True	False
3-XHTML is case sensitive.	True	False
4-The <!DOCTYPE> tag needs to be closed.	True	False

5-List the three types of DTD.

6-Which tag is not correct (not self-closing)?

**
**

<hr />

<img />

<input />

<select />

7- This attribute, *<option selected="selected" />*, is not correct.	True	False

8- Correct this tag: *<table border=2 cellspacing =5> </table>*

9- What is the result of this statement? <table border="3" frame="**rhs**">

10-What this does this statement do, **<select> <option> ... </option> </select>**?

11- The <legend> tag must be declared within *fieldset*.	True	False

Answer

1- eXtensible HyperText Markup Language

2- True

3- True

4- False

5- **Strict**, **Transitional**, and **Frameset**.

6- <select> </select>

7- False

8-The correct tag is *<table border="2" cellspacing="5"> </table>*

9- Creates right-hand-side border.

10- Creates drop-down-list

11- True

Appendix

Some important HTML & CSS to be remembered

1- HTML declaring fonts and colors

<basefont> </basefont>	Kipping the same font for entire texts
<font></font>	Change the font
<font size ="2"> </font>	Size of font =2 points
<font color="red">	Change color to red
<font face="Arial"> </font>	Uses family font = Arial

2- Hexadecimal examples

Decimal	0	1	2	3	4	5	6	7	8	9	10	11	12	13	14	15
Hexadecimal	0	1	2	3	4	5	6	7	8	9	A	B	C	D	E	F

The letter **F** is the maximum number which represents the white color like: #FFFFFF.
To convert the hexadecimal to the decimal number use this formula.
(Letter * 16)+ Letter
Therefore **#FFFFFF** is (15 * 16) + 15=255 so the #FFFFFF is (255,255, 255)
Another example:
Convert **#DC143C** to decimal.
DC= (13 * 16) +12 =220
14= (1 *16) + 4=20
3C= (3*16) + 12=60
It becomes (220, 20, 60)

3- Font size CSS
◆ **<absolute-size>**
◆ **<relative-size>**
◆ **<length>**
◆ **<percentage**

4- Font groups

CSS Font size groups			
Length group	**Absolute group**	**Relative group**	**Percentage group**
font-size: normal font-size:10px font-size:12pt	font-size:x-small font-size:xx-small font-size:small font-size:medium font-size:large font-size:x-large font-size:xx-large	font-size:smaller font-size:larger	font-size:50%

pt (points; 1pt=1/72in)
pc (picas; 1pc=12pt)
em (the height of the element's font)
px (pixels)
Please note, "pt" is a print unit, and not a exact screen unit.
Fonts can be manipulated by these features: font-size, font-style, font-variant, font-weight, line-height, and font-family.

5- HTML entities

HTML Entities			
Character	**Entity**	**Decimal**	**Result**
quotation mark	&quot;	&#34;	"
ampersand	&amp;	&#38;	&
less-than sign	&lt;	&#60;	<
greater-than sign	&gt;	&#62;	>
euro sign	&euro;	&#8364;	€
copyright sign	&copy;	&#169;	©

6- Image extensions

Extension	Name	Description
.gif	Graphics Interchange Format	This graphics file format used by the CompuServe in the late 1980. GIF supports 256 color monitors. I this an easy image to be used in WWW.
.jpg or **.jpeg**	Joint Photographic Experts Group	Data compression for color images especially used for photos and scanning. The jpg size is smaller compare to gif. It is familiar for most browsers.
.png	Portable Network	This new graphics format is similar to the GIF. It

	Graphics	designed to be replacing to the gif. Presently all browsers are handling it well.
.bmp	BitMaPped graphic	This graphics format used in the Windows. It can be simply created by MS-paint. We usually do not use .bmp on image for internet but some parts like counter is in bmp format.

7- List of some important browsers

Mozila FireFox	Mozilla is an open source projects, including Firefox, Minimo Mobile Browser. It comes from old Netscape.
Microsoft Internet Explorer (IE)	Come from Microsoft
Konqueror	Unix-based Web browser
Safari	KHTML-based web for Apple Computers and optimized for Mac OS X.
Opera	Browser support for **BitTorren**t, with multiple search engines.

8- Declaration of selector

Selector	Property	Value
P	{ color :	blue ; }

9- Fonts Property

Property	Example
font-family	font-family : arial, san-serif
font-size	font-size: normal font-size:10px (pixel size) font-size:12pt (point size) **Relative size :** font-size:small font-size:x-small font-size:xx-small font-size:smaller font-size:medium font-size:large font-size:x-large font-size:xx-large font-size:larger font-size:55%
font-style	font-style:normal font-style:italic font-style:oblique

font-weight	font-weight:normal font-weight:bold font-weight:bolder font-weight:lighter **font-weight:100**

- If the font-family made up of two parts like Arial narrow then you should place it into quotation like: font-family: "Arial narrow".
- The font-weight can be between 100 to 900.
- Normal=400 and bold=700

10- Text color & backgrounds

To color text background:	**div.textBack1 { background-color: gray; }**
Text foreground:	**div.textColor{ color: " #0000ff " }**
You can use the RGB value:	**div.textColor{ color:rgb(0 0 255) }**
To color page background:	**body { background-color: yellow; }**

11- Border property

Properties	Values	Example
border-bottom-width **border-left-width** **border-width** **border-top-width** **border-right-width**	thin , medium , thick, length	border-bottom-width: thin
border-top-color **border-right-color** **border-bottom-color** **border-left-color** **border-color**	Any color, Use rgb, color name or hexadecimal value	border-right-color : blue or border-bottom-color : #CCCCCC
border-bottom-style **border-left-style** **border-style** **border-top-style** **border-right-style**	none , solid , double , groove , ridge , inset , outset You can use combination of both like: solid double or bauble solid.	border-right-style: groove border-style: dotted border-style: hidden border-style: solid
border-top **border-right** **border-bottom** **border-left** **border**	*border-width, border-style, border-color*	border-bottom: thick inset yellow

12- Text properties

Properties	Value	Example
letter-spacing	normal , *length*	letter-spacing:4pt
vertical-align	sub , super	vertical-align:sub
text-decoration	none , underline, overline , line-through	text-decoration:none
text-transform	capitalize , uppercase , lowercase , none	text-transform: lowercase
text-align	left , right , center , justify	text-align: center
text-indent	*length* , *percentage*	text-indent:10px
line-height	normal , *number* , *length* , *percentage*	line-height:normal
white-space	normal ,pre, nowrap	White-space:normal

13- List Properties

Property	Value	Example
list-style-position	inside outside	ol { list-style-position:inside; } ul { list-style-position:outside; }
list-style-image	URL	ul { list-style-image:url(image1.jpg); }
list-style	Can declare multiple attributes list-style-type list-style-position list-style-image	ul { list-style:disc inside url(image.gif); }
marker-offset	auto	ol:before { display:marker; marker-offset:3px; }
list-style-type	disc circle square decimal decimal-leading-zero lower-roman upper-roman lower-alpha upper-alpha lower-greek lower-latin upper-latin hebrew	ol { list-style-type: lower-latin; } ul { list-style-type:circle; }

armenian georgian cjk-ideographic hiragana katakana hiragana-iroha katakana-iroha	

14- Table Properties in CSS

Property	Value
border-collapse	collapse separate
border-spacing	length length
caption-side	top bottom left right
empty-cell	show hide
table-layout	auto fixed

15- Links:

A:link is used for a new link.
A:visited is used for visited link.
A:active is used for activate the link when you click on it.
A:hover is used for mouse over the link (e.g. changes color).

Text decorations

text-decoration:none means no decoration around the selected text
text-decoration:underline return a underline bar
text-decoration:overline return an over line bar
text-decoration:line-through return a bar through the text
text-decoration:blink return blinking but does not work under IE

16- Margin properties

Margin Properties		
Properties	**Value**	**Example**
margin-top	length , percentage , auto	margin-top:5px
margin-bottom		margin-bottom:5em
margin-left		margin-left:5pt
margin-right		margin-right:5px
margin		margin: 15px 5px 10px 15px

17- Overflow:

Overflow properties	
Visible	default
Hidden	Does not display scrollbar
Auto	Automatic display of scroll when text is large
Scroll	Display scrollbar

18- Filter effects

Filter name	Effect
Filter: alpha	Create opacity that becomes light by the end
Filter: blur	Creates blur object
Filter: chroma	Works with image, makes transparent
Filter: dropshadow	Create dropping shadow along X and y with specified color
Filter: glow	Creates some glows around the object
Filter: shadow	Something between *dropshadow* and glow
Filter: flipH	Flipping horizontally
Filter: flipV	Flipping vertically
Filter: grayscale	Convert color to shaded gray
Filter: wave	Creates wave shape of an object
Filter: xray	Grayscale color kind of x-ray image
Filter: invert	Create the negative or opposite site of the color number
Filter: mask	Shift transparent to specified color

Words Search

Printed in the United Kingdom
by Lightning Source UK Ltd.
127835UK00003B/244/A